PATTERN

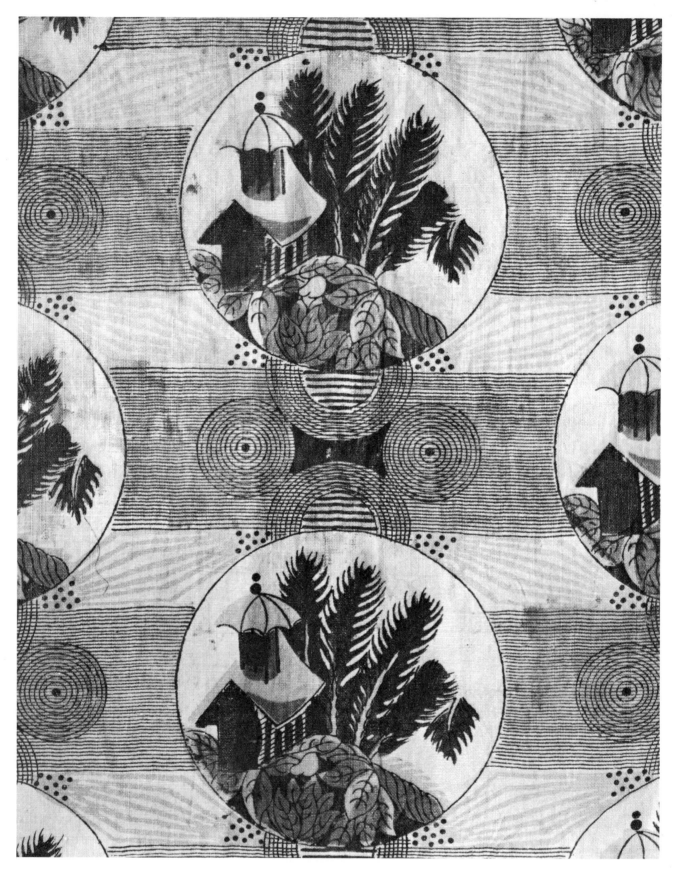

Frontispiece. Printed cotton, first half of the nineteenth century, English or American. A truly "enigmatic" pattern that could be put in any of the book's eight categories except under Animals or Figures.

PATTERN

A Historical Panorama

William Justema

New York Graphic Society   Boston

To Hans Dorfer

First Edition

T 07/76

Library of Congress Cataloging in Publication Data

Justema, William, 1904–
  Pattern.

  Bibliography: p.
  Includes index.
  1. Design, Decorative — Themes, motives — History.
I. Title.
NK1520.J87   745.4   76-8451
ISBN 0-8212-0665-6

New York Graphic Society books are published by Little, Brown and Company
Published simultaneously in Canada by Little, Brown and Company (Canada) Limited

Printed in the United States of America

Contents

A Note of Thanks

For their graciousness, imagination, vigilance, or skill I am particularly indebted to these individuals: Lisa Taylor, director, and Christian Rohlfing, administrator, The Cooper–Hewitt Museum of Design, New York, Smithsonian Institution; Judith Tankard; Robin Bledsoe, editor, New York Graphic Society; Jean Mailey and Janet Thorpe, The Metropolitan Museum of Art; Christa C. Mayer-Thurman, The Art Institute of Chicago; Petronel Lukens, The Textile Museum, Washington, D.C.; Ross E. Taggart, Nelson Gallery of Art–Atkins Museum, Kansas City, Missouri; Donna Benders, designer, Little, Brown and Company; Kristen Chiara, draftsman; Tom Bockelman and Allen Short, photographers.

Introduction

From the standpoint of *design*, any meaningful classification in the decorative arts seems, at first, a hopeless task. Time (or chronology) and place (or provenance) seldom give the kind of visual information that practicing designers or an interested public require, and classification according to *materials* or *techniques* is equally unrevealing. The same is true — to an extent — of *subject-matter*. Even when the subject of a design is beyond question (and is restricted to a single subject), the *treatment* of a design can range anywhere from extreme realism to extreme abstraction, and, in so doing, suggest other categories than the one chosen.

Yet we have to begin somewhere. Although it has never been officially recognized as such, there does exist within the design industry a rudimentary way of grouping designs *according to the impression they create*. I was always aware of these tacit divisions during the forty-odd years I was engaged in designing wallpapers and textiles; only recently have I clarified and systematized them for general use in the Pattern and Motif Archive which is one of the features of the Library Complex at the newly constituted Cooper-Hewitt Museum of Design, Smithsonian Institution, in New York City.

When a designer needs a motif he is typically in a hurry. He rarely has time to develop a motif from scratch. Indeed, there is but the slightest chance that, by doing so, he will come up with anything strikingly original. Pattern design — like every other art form — is based on the work of the many centuries that preceded it. There have been numerous attempts to classify and to create patterns chiefly by *geometrical* means (and, as regards creation, many of these have been brilliant, notably in the medieval Islamic world). But as a practical, all-purpose approach to an understanding of patterns, it is more expedient to realize that every pattern, whatever its superficial aspect, utilizes one or the other of *two basic types of repeat: the "block" or the "brick."* Once the few variations of these are understood, a pattern designer is free to start from any suggestion that appeals to him: a flower or a façade — the points of departure are infinite.

In this book, for the most part, we will limit ourselves to patterns and motifs that are accomplished facts. Since, as such, they are automatically protected by copyright (according to their priority), *none of them may be reproduced for commercial purposes exactly as it appears*. However, and as if to acknowledge the truism that no design is entirely original, the copyright laws demand only a token amount of modification. Generally speaking, this is no more than the change of *scale* or the degree of *coverage* a designer would wish to make, anyway, in order to give an old pattern (or motif) a fresh appearance. (And it is always wise to admit the source, as it will inevitably be found out.)

By now you will have noticed that our subject has its own fairly distinctive vocabulary. To facilitate checking up, all the requisite words can be found in the Index, but it will be pleasanter and more instructive to become familiar with the language of pattern and design as you encounter its special terms either in the historical review that follows; in the text preceding each section of Part II; or, better still, in the commentary that accompanies most of the illustrations, for that's where you will see the words in question demonstrated.

These eight sections, listed in the Table of Contents, are of course the "categories" that are based on the broad classifications long assumed by the professional designers, stylists, and manufacturers throughout the textile, wallcovering, and floorcovering industries: businesses that adopted pattern in order to enhance their product. Within each category patterns of the same sort are, whenever possible, grouped in subdivisions — with reference made to other categories or subdivisions if such connections seem logical or provocative.

But prior to that the book begins with a general introduction, "Motifs and the Repeat." Besides making explicit distinctions between overly familiar terms, and between the manners in which geometrical and naturalistic motifs function, it refers in passing to various age-old forms of repetition, and, on pages 10 and 11 a series of diagrams and examples shows that the most complicated-looking repeats are basically simple. It can't be said too often. With so many people dependent on some aspect of pattern for their living, one would expect a good deal of knowledge or curiosity about the *structure* of pattern, which, after all, is its salient quality.

Such is not the case. After the five or six thousand centuries during which designer-craftsmen have made patterns, the mechanics of pattern construction not only remain strangely mysterious, but the world's more ingenious pattern-makers are an anonymous legion — since no single person, unaided, could have created the more extraordinary examples (such as the guilloche). In this respect they resemble the group efforts of prehistoric cave painting, and bear comparison to today's large-scale architectural projects, which are worked out on a hundred drafting tables along the lines of a dozen precedents. An individual signature is seldom more than the sign of a culmination, or, in recent times, of an advertising "promotion."

Although all the patterns illustrated here are noteworthy for one reason or another, few of them are put forward as major works of art. Instead, they are a carefully selected cross section of pattern-making (or the *makings* of pattern) through the ages, together with a generous sampling of what the contemporary marketplace has produced. To this extent they constitute both a summary and a forecast, because some of the physical aspects of pattern will unquestionably change. A spectacular use of images projected by colored light can be expected, as also an increase in optical illusions and — when time and talent permit — subjects that transform themselves into other subjects à la Maurits Escher (1898–1972). Nonetheless, pattern will essentially remain a single unit of design repeated over and over again, and nothing in the future should truly surprise anyone who thoughtfully peruses these pages.

"Sky and Water," *above*, was a diamond-shaped drawing by M. C. Escher that has been made rectangular. If the metamorphosis of fishes and birds were continued, at both top and bottom, a horizontally banded pattern would result.

"Arabesque," *above*, has been selected by way of credentials. It was the author's first big-selling wallpaper, and was exhibited in this room setting by T. H. Robsjohn-Gibbings at the Katzenbach & Warren showroom, New York, in 1938. Originally made by the hand-print silk-screen process, the pattern was soon transferred to mechanical roller printing.

I Motifs and the Repeat

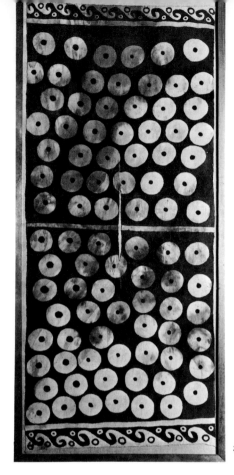

3

4

There is seemingly no end to the confusion that the word "pattern" engenders. Dictionaries are of little help. They stress metal molds and "models made for imitation," quite forgetting the demure idea of patterns also being the shaped tissue papers used in home dressmaking. Scholars are even less helpful. The eminent English archaeologist Joan Evans, in an imposing two-volume work entitled *Pattern: A Study of Ornament in Western Europe from 1180 to 1900*, referred to the shadows cast by leaves on the walls around her as "patterns" that gave her as much pleasure as the artifacts and architectural remains she was studying. Surfaces patterned by chance are undeniably attractive, but since Dr. Evans's theme was the evolution of specific design motifs — few of which relied on repetition — her frequent poetic effusions, plus a vague use of the word "pattern," cast shadows of their own on her considerable scholarship.

Putting the love of nature temporarily to one side (for it is notoriously hazardous to research, even of my workaday sort), there are a number of key words we should weigh: the first four being *decoration, ornament, design,* and, of course, *pattern.* True, the word "decoration" has been somewhat nullified, of late, by interior decorators choosing to call themselves interior *designers,* but as it appears to be a distinction without a difference, this question can remain in limbo until we learn to what extent interior designers actually design; not simply make selections of furnishings and then arrange them. Meanwhile the terms "decoration" and "ornament" are virtually interchangeable, though the latter may be preferred for a single object (e.g., a Grinling Gibbons carving), the former for a large project (e.g., a Tiepolo ceiling).

If only "design" and "pattern" could be separated with such dispatch! The trouble, naturally, is that "design" has come into general use for anything that's planned, whereas "pattern" — if it is to make any sense in the visual arts at all — must be confined to a limited field and its products. This means that while design, as verb and as noun, can range far and wide, embracing almost every conceivable activity and result, pattern must evolve from a single source, adding to itself as a coral reef does, with each additional shape related to the one it grew from, so to speak. These shaped areas give us several more words of key importance. Thus: a *motif* may be a design that is complete in itself, but in relation to *pattern* design, is best thought of as one of the *units* that makes up a *repeat — the repeat being the type of repetition that makes a pattern a pattern.* Does it sound rather esoteric? Possibly it does, at first. But every art form has special disciplines, and these — once understood and accepted — yield literally endless visual pleasure. In an earlier book I said that *"good patterns* [by which I meant an aggregate of motifs] *gain, rather than lose, by being repeated."* There is, moreover, the satisfaction of knowing that although a pattern can loosely be

PERU AND THE SCHOOL OF PARIS. *Opposite, above,* section of a painted cotton garment "probably Early Chimu" (ca. A.D. 1000). *Opposite, below,* simplified drawing of the door to the Confession at the Chapel of the Rosary, Vence, France, designed about 1949 by Matisse. Far from being odious, the comparison of similar shapes and spacing can be illuminating.

referred to as a "design," only a design that meets certain requirements can correctly be called a "pattern."

From our present position in history we can merely speculate upon the probable beginnings of pattern. The most persuasive arguments are advanced by the "art in industry" school. Followers of this credo believe that our decorative motifs originated, little by little, in the weaving of rush mats, the stitching of animal skins into garments and shelters, and in the trial-and-error processes incidental to making pottery. In their opinion these domestic activities (i.e., home "industries") gradually produced the checkerboard and zigzag motifs, the key meander, and eventually led to such sophisticated motifs as the spiral, the swastika, and the interwoven bands we call the guilloche. If this is true — and there is no proof to the contrary — the symbolical origins that another group of scholars favors were, on the whole, an afterthought. Indeed, many anthropologists report that while most primitive craftsmen still alive attach some "meaning" to the symbols they use, they often disagree as to what the symbols signify.

Regardless of how the motifs of pattern originated, it is clear that *the repeat developed with them.* If all-over angular patterning resulted from the weaving of varicolored rush mats, the impulsive decoration of pottery may well have given birth to the continuous border and even be responsible for a number of curved motifs that — in the late Stone and early Bronze Ages — could be painted, incised, or hammered, but not woven. Then these borders, by the overlay and extension at right angles that yesterday's designers knew as "crossbanding," might have established the essentials of the repeat at least as early as 2000 B.C., when many Egyptian tombs were decorated with elaborately patterned ceilings. Here, without recourse to a discussion of lotus or papyrus (considered mandatory in any analysis of Egyptian art), there is ample evidence that nature and geometry had been successfully fused. In fact Mesopotamia, and, later, Greece, may be said to have regressed to simple spot and banded patterns. The rows of glazed brick or carved stone rosettes we find from Babylon to Persepolis, and the Greek use of the acanthus, the palmette, and the anthemion or honeysuckle motif, architecturally or on vases, lack the sophistication, as pattern, which Egypt had attained. This is understandable; Greek artists were preoccupied with the human body and its idealized realism.

Rome was not. A culture dedicated to conquest, it exaggerated to a gross degree the artistic influences it encountered, and for no easily explained reason found one of its most successful expressions in mosaic pavement. Optical illusions had been explored since prehistoric times, but never with such virtu-

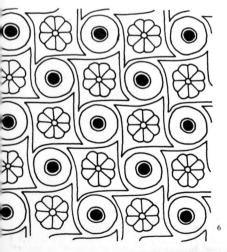

SOME ANCIENT MOTIFS. *Above, left,* the guilloche had become a favorite border decoration in Assyria by the 7th century B.C. *Below left,* a popular decoration for Egyptian tombs. *Opposite, above,* a "Celtic" Knot. *Opposite, below,* part of a Roman pavement that may or may not be related to the other motifs.

osity. For our purpose the more pictorial floors with mythological subjects (as at Ostia) are of little interest, but the geometrical invention on view in museums throughout the world leads to a tantalizing question. Did Roman pavements spread a knowledge of the "Greek" key, the swastika, the guilloche, and other interlace motifs as widely as they seem to have done? Many scholars answer yes. To all appearances Imperial Rome cultivated a taste for the kind of abstract geometrical design that has proved to be universal: equally at home in primitive societies from Oceania to Africa as well as in modern art. From the seventh century onward the new monasteries of Ireland and England made what is perhaps the most striking and exquisite use of it. What would the Book of Kells, the Book of Durrow, the Gospel of Lindisfarne be without their large illuminated initials, their rich "carpet pages"? We can almost see the monks who were visiting around the shores of the Mediterranean hoist up their habits and return with all prudent speed to their northern scriptoria. There they discreetly added the tiny heads of animals, out of deference, perhaps, to pagan neighbors.

Islam's contribution to the geometric spirit was markedly different, considering that it, too, was nurtured by religious fervor. For although Celtic interlace and Islamic grillwork have an oriental opulence in common, one covers the surface out of sheer exuberance; the other keeps its style under control (as at the Alhambra) by calculation. Before conquering half the then-known world — beginning with the death of Mohammed in A.D. 632 — the Arabs had been rug-weaving nomads, and the arab-esques they left behind them in the mosques and pleasure-domes of the Near East, India, North Africa, and Spain were based on an appreciation of mathematics they had gained from the desert stars. Still another type of geometrical pattern-making occurs in the fretwork of China. Because it can possess great subtlety, we are inclined to believe Daniel Sheets Dye when, in his book *A Grammar of Chinese Lattices*, he writes that Chinese frets can be traced to around 1000 B.C., and despite their many divisions into "windwheel," "ice-ray," and other descriptive classes, all schemes and proportions were committed to memory and passed on from one "master carpenter" to another.

It will be obvious that in the groups of patterns we have just considered, the entire structure being framework, *motifs and repeats are inseparable:* in the best of them, indeed, form and content have a degree of unity found only in the purest music and architecture. Such economy is hardly possible when patterns employ naturalistic subject matter. Forgetting what they might have learned from their ancestors, the Coptic Christians of Egypt began what amounted, in the western world, to a long struggle to create patterns after models that were veritable pictures. No one can resist naïveté, and these little Hellenistic figure and animal tapestries were, and are, quite unsurpassed in charm. Unfortunately their avowed purpose as spot ornaments on tunics was overlooked by later cultures; they were never intended to be repeating patterns. As a consequence the

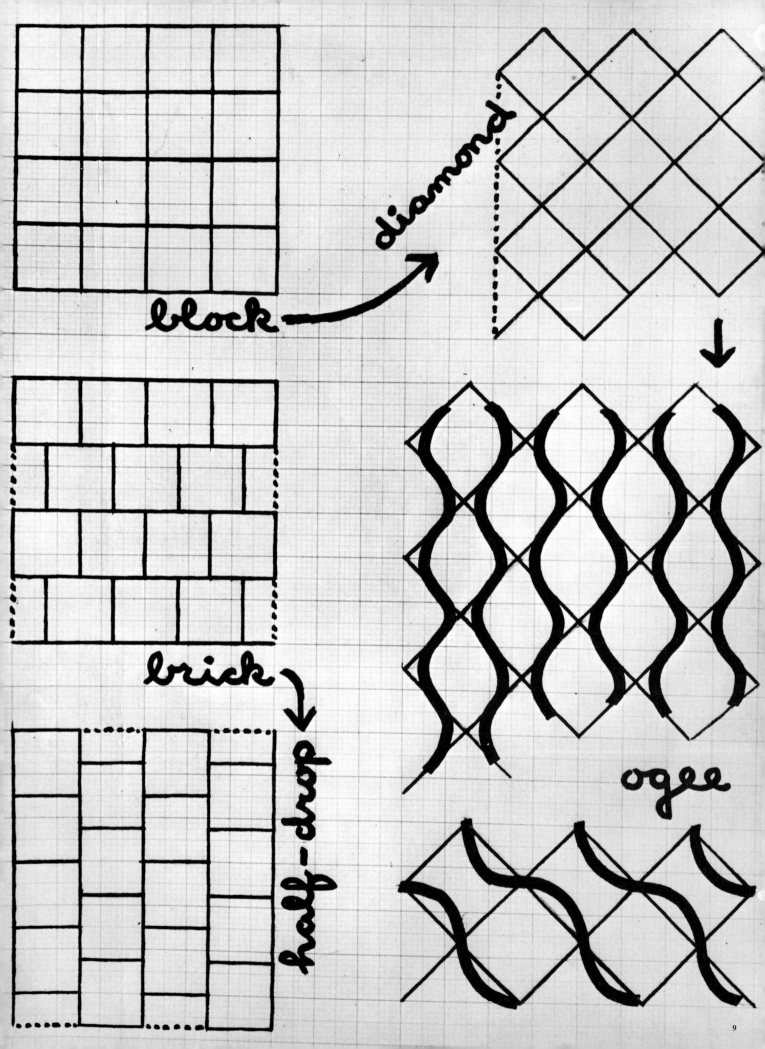

block

diamond

brick

half-drop

ogee

9

10

11

12

THE REPEAT AND HOW IT WORKS. *Opposite*, the block and the brick repeat —
sometimes called "the straight match" and "the drop" — and the form they take by being
turned to a 45- or a 90-degree angle, their ogival or serpentine forms being made by
drawing lines through, or around, what are basically only two positions. *Above*, portions
of three historical patterns suggest how diverse an impression these repeats can give when
put into practice. The tiles are from the recent excavations in China, the "scale" or
imbricated print is from 18th-century France, and the ogival leaves are on a piece of
16th-century Florentine cut velvet in the Musée des Arts Decoratifs, Paris.

11

13

14

15

16

circles and squares that framed almost all Coptic ornament were imposed on the more magnificent Byzantine textiles for centuries.

Certainly the Egyptian Copts should not be blamed for this development. The stylistic conventions that, in my opinion, they touched off were partly due to the limited weaving techniques at the time, and are partly explained by New Rome's love of pomp and ceremony. Both factors were soon reaffirmed. When, during the first few centuries of greater Byzantium (the core of which, at Constantinople, lasted miraculously from A.D. 330 until its final fall to the Turks in 1453), the drawloom superseded tapestry, its mechanical advantages were somewhat ignored. Stiffly symmetrical designs prevailed, both to save labor — for a design could be divided in two halves by a simple reversal or "overturn" of the thread sequence — and also to maintain the formal balance that, in the western mind, connotes power. The connection between technical progress and what patrons desire is more than fortuitous; they invariably go hand in hand. If to technique and the taste that accompanies it we add human curiosity — our perennial interest in the exotic — we have all the ingredients that contribute to pattern, and the changes it undergoes.

But we must be wary of quick conclusions. No sooner do we ascribe symmetry to western design, asymmetry to eastern, than we discover a hundred indigenous patterns that contradict us. Prior to the nineteenth century, which kept a wealth of records we have access to, many textile attributions are qualified by the word "probably," for they frequently depend upon appearances. That these can be deceitful is shown by the alacrity with which the Orient and the Occident can, when they choose, absorb each other's influences. Not only Sassanian Persia (A.D. 224–650) but the whole East poured decorative devices into what, for convenience, I have labeled "Byzantine" silks, yet it is not until the fourteenth century at Lucca, Italy, that fantastic motifs and discontinuous diagonal lines of repeat allow us to say definitely that "chinoiserie" has arrived. Even so, in the Renaissance that followed, a typical pattern was the so-called pomegranate, formal and symmetrical. In her valuable book *Two Thousand Years of Textiles* Adèle Coulin Weibel writes, "The pomegranate pattern of the Renaissance had its beginnings thousands of years earlier. The original lotus motif of early Egyptian art was changed into the more conventional palmette and used, side by side with the naturalistic pine-cone pattern, in Assyria, and thus inherited by Persia and Greece. Transplanted to China, it was reborn there as a more or less realistic lotus and as such incorporated into Islamic art. Thence it

ISLAMIC ARABESQUE. *Opposite,* in the diagram at the upper left we see how Mohammedan craftsmen arrived at the frets and lattices that constitute their major contribution to pattern design. On a network of divided circles they chose points between which lines were drawn to create a seemingly endless variety of linear grilles. See also pages 186 and 191. These drawings are from the folio *Les Eléments de l'Art Arabe* by J. Bourgoin, published by the Librarie de Fermin-Didot et Cie, Paris, 1879.

was brought to Italy, where it continued in full blossom all through the Gothic period. The Renaissance and the Baroque brought the long evolution to a triumphant end" — with vaguely fruitlike centers, I might add, surrounded by acanthus leaves and lined up in compartments like prize cabbages

Cheap cynicism? That may be, but it is the inevitable reaction of a contemporary pattern-maker who is wearied and sickened by the "damask" designs that have been dominant in home furnishings in the United States for over half a century. To a sociologist this should be indicative of America's innate, quite Byzantine, conservatism. There are fortunately (for art's sake) nearly four hundred years between us and the High Renaissance, and in that lengthy span, and especially in the seventeenth and eighteenth centuries, pattern design became creative again — as we will note in the texts and see in the pictures that follow. Patterns are a true mirror of their times. In 1517, when Martin Luther nailed his Ninety-five Theses on the door of the castle church in Wittenburg, he not only challenged the Catholic hierarchy but the hypocrisy of the Renaissance as a whole. By precipitating the Baroque and then the Rococo period, the Reformation freed Europe of a number of stultifying conventions that had long been accruing. Not the least of these was the tradition of historical pattern. As we know, the Renaissance mistook Roman copies for Greek originals; it was a culture built on misunderstandings. The eighteenth century may not have been as "enlightened" as it believed itself to be, but it made brilliant use of every foreign influence, refreshed itself by observing nature, and scored tremendous advances in the mechanical means so necessary to keeping pattern design alive. Machine-printed fabrics and rolls of wallpaper were perfected in the eighteenth century, the Jacquard loom immediately afterward.

Repeats remained what they had always been. They are diagrammed on page 10. Although patterned surfaces may become enormously complicated — and consist of several "layers" — the individual units that are made up of one or more motifs can be repeated in only two ways, of which there are limited variations. Some of the Bizarre silks at the end of the seventeenth century and a handful of Art Nouveau patterns at the end of the nineteenth seem, by their strange extravagance, to escape the "block" or the "brick" repeat, but, on analysis, their freedom is more apparent than real. It may require actual physical change from one subject to another to achieve an additional kind of repeat. I touched on this possibility at the conclusion of the Introduction, mentioning the Dutch artist M. C. Escher, in whose "periodic" patterns one image — a fish, say — goes through a gradual metamorphosis and becomes another — a bird — without any conspicuous break. On a visit to Europe in the late 1960s I wanted to pay tribute to the most original designer of our century and discuss this and related matters, but learned that Escher was gravely ill. A brain affliction had reached its last stages.

II Eight Categories of Pattern

16

ANIMALS IN DESIGN. *Above*, "Man on Donkey," cotton roller printed in colors for the Portuguese market, England, about 1850. *Opposite*, a lion-dragon from an unidentified textile possibly woven in late medieval Italy. While the yardage above could almost be classed as a Scenic, the hybrid animal opposite was definitely a heraldic emblem. These extremes of realism and fantasy occur in each of our eight categories.

18

1 Animals

19

MIRROR SYMMETRY. A panel of damask "probably Spanish, 17th century." Notice the many animals needed to fill the space around the dominant leopards, and that — to facilitate drawloom production — one side of the material exactly "reflects" or reverses the other side, divided only by the immemorial device of upright foliage.

"A" is for animals, and by coincidence they appear to have been prehistoric man's first subject matter. But it would be too much to expect the alphabet and a chronological account to remain parallel, and we have chosen to list the categories of pattern noncommittally, in alphabetical order, not because animals are the earliest subjects we know of — and in any case the cave paintings of northern Spain are illustrations rather than designs — but because an alphabetical listing does not give one type of pattern undue prominence. Knowing how fashions change, I would be foolish to reflect current preferences (namely the close competition at present between floral and geometrical subjects in what the English call "furnishing" materials), well aware that, at any season, all figuration could be declared anathema, and only plain textures find favor. Nonetheless, in a determined effort to be as methodical as possible, we have adopted, within each category, a roughly chronological order, sometimes with curious results.

One of these was hinted at in the introduction. I said there that "the *treatment* of a design can range anywhere from extreme realism to extreme abstraction." To this I might have added, "and it may sometimes be hard to tell whether realism or abstraction came first." And how could it be otherwise, with the history of art keeping such a capricious timetable? After the Renaissance the average educated person was convinced that the one inviolable standard of artistic excellence was the idealized realism of the Greeks. Then see what happened. Less than a century ago the discovery of academic-looking prehistoric painting coincided with the emergence of what is still called Modern Art. Add African sculpture to the mixture, as the Cubists did, and intellectual chaos reigns. If an image drawn thirty centuries ago on the walls of a cave in Spain or France and a fetish carved a few decades ago in the Congo are equal in esthetic value (as many believe) to a Leonardo or a Donatello — what price progress? what price decline?

Animal subjects, as such, were never the issue. Few artists have declared themselves regarding prehistoric art: they've left that to the scientists who, in more senses than one, have had themselves a field day. It is only recently, when the enthusiasm of the ethnologists for their theories of "sympathetic magic," "shaman societies," and "amazing spatial concepts" has slightly abated, that the public can judge for itself the actual success of cave art, and this quite conveniently, by visiting an excellent replica of Altamira's large Hall of Animals in a museum nearly next door to the Prado. The difficulty of animal representation at once becomes obvious: the need for quiet subjects, a rapid medium, or great skill. Failing these, we find several monuments to communal effort, or, as at Lascaux, a few dazzling impressions among much childish daubing. Cave art belongs to Science, after all. Millennia were to pass before animal subject matter was perfected (as at Nineveh and Luristan) and it may be significant that the most expressive figures of what is called the "Second Hunters' Style" — discovered on more exposed sites in the Spanish Levant and North Africa, and dated some ten thousand years later than the caves — are human rather than animal.

Without question it is the sheer difficulty of drawing animals realistically that accounts for the admirable tendency to stylize them. Hence their prevalence in the crafts; no one expects verisimilitude in weaving or ceramics. Leaving the equivocal achievements at Altamira and Lascaux far behind, the artists of the Bronze Age stalked animal subjects with exemplary caution. What we call "abstraction" became a deliberate practice, the earliest examples in any quantity being the animal masks on the ceremonial bronzes of Shang-Yin China (1500–1000 B.C.). To quote the first impression they made on me: "These bronzes are among the great designing curiosities of all time. Reversing the usual process of natural objects becoming stylized, theirs is a bestiary made up of odd 'hooks' and partial frets, of circular mounds and squared spirals that suddenly come alive. Viewed at close range, without knowing what to look for, the handsome green-black surfaces seem to be covered with abstract figures in low relief, generously incised. Moving back, one sees something else. A strange face stares out: the *t'ao-t'tieh* or heraldic animal mask. If one wishes, some of these faces can be identified as tigers by whisker shapes, or as rams or buffaloes by their horns, but for the most part they fall, like dragons, into the category of imaginary animals . . ." and I am reminded that, aside from horses, lions, and the two-headed eagle (said to look simultaneously East and West!), most of the animals and birds in ancient art were imaginary hybrids: the griffin, the hippogriff, the phoenix, and the Chinese "unicorn" or *kh'i-lin*, to name the principal ones.

But because such animals are so composite, and so liable to change character, it is impossible to decide just when the dragon motif, for instance, assumed a recognizable form. Jade pendants from the Shang-Yin Dynasty, though said to represent dragons, are little more than curves with claws attached, and the larger, figured-S motifs of fourteenth- and fifteenth-century Armenian "dragon" rugs can scarcely be distinguished from what are said to be clouds or foliage. We will experience the same uncertainty in the next chapter with the "puma" or "jaguar" tapestries of the Tiahuanaco period of Peru (A.D. 700–1000); except for the eyes we can't be sure what the parts are. In their abstraction these Peruvian designs are so closely related to the *t'ao-t'tieh* masks of China as to reinforce the notion that people from Asia might long ago have come across the Bering Strait to settle on the western coast of Central and South America.

All told, animal subjects make a strange story. The creatures that have provided man with food, sport, and companionship have fared better in his major arts than in his lesser ones. In pattern design they doubtless reached their peak when Byzantium and the early Middle Ages put them, usually in pairs, within enclosures, either rampant and confronted (face to face) or addorsed (back to back). As individual motifs, animals were useful to heraldry but have proved

recalcitrant to later-day designers — except for the ingenious, sedulous M. C. Escher — perhaps because of the patience required to fit them into a logical scheme (and it must be admitted that many of Escher's patterns are decidedly unpleasant). Looking back on their incomparable history, it would seem that animal motifs, with all their vital potential, have thus far been of the greatest interest when they were subdued by abstraction and were least like themselves.

"Butterfly Chariot," a drawing in opaque watercolors for an embroidered border, artist unknown, France, about 1780. Because of its oriental connotations, James McNeill Whistler took the butterfly for his hallmark, and it continually enlivens patterns, as on pages 44, 45, and 98.

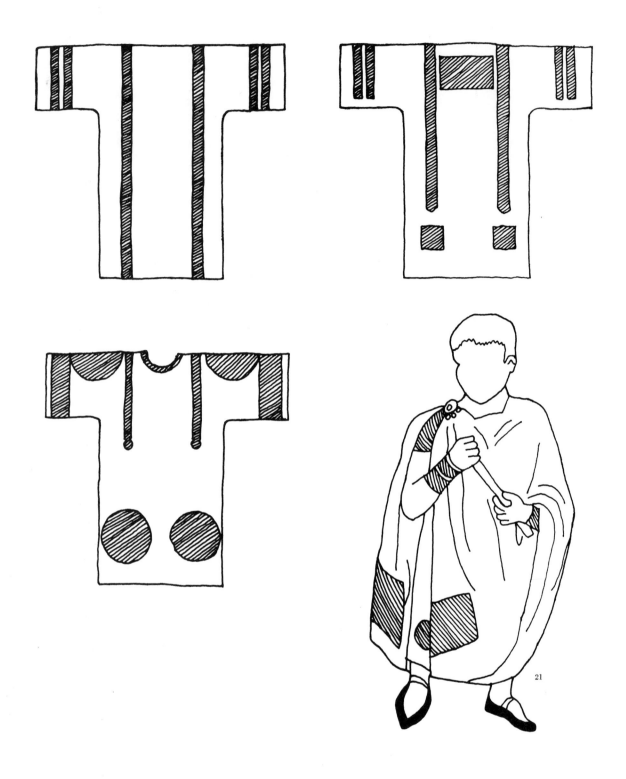

ORNAMENT MAKES THE MAN. *Above*, four sketches for Coptic garments from Lili Blumenthal's *Creative Design in Wall Hangings* (Crown, 1967). *Opposite, above*, a small Coptic tapestry from the 6th century, once a tunic decoration. *Opposite, below*, a "rank badge" from 20th-century Korea, obviously equivalent to China's "mandarin squares" that go back to the Ming Dynasty (1368–1644).

22

23

ENCLOSED ANIMALS. *Above,* confronted lions in a sawtooth roundel, attributed by Otto von Falke to 12th-century Lucca, Italy. *Opposite,* an "armorial damask" from late 16th-century Italy or Spain. Caged animals are usually simplified and quite formal.

THE ANIMALS ESCAPE. *Above left*, detail of leopards, "peacocks," and griffins embroidered in gold within scalloped circles and diamonds on a silk dossal from 14th-century Germany. *Above right*, brocaded dragons and kh'i-lins from 14th-century Lucca, Italy. *Above, right of center*, gazelles printed on linen from late 12th-century Germany. *Opposite, above*, stags in the "rays of glory" typical of 14th-century Lucca. *Opposite, below*, a towel woven with winged dragons in Perugia, Italy, during the 15th century.

28

29

30

31

32

28

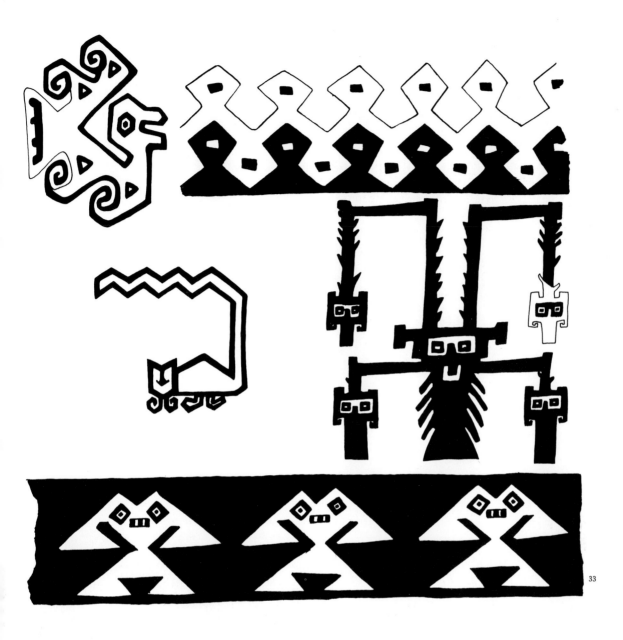

33

GROTESQUE AND FANTASTIC. *Opposite, above,* a drawing of Bosch-like creatures from Flanders, 1550–75. *Opposite, below,* a 17th to 18th-century embroidered band of imaginary animals by a fountain, from Azemur, Morocco. *Above,* five motifs from pre-Columbian Peru that include serpents' heads, a lobster, and, at the bottom, what are said to be fish.

A SIMIAN WORLD. *Above,* apes on a printed batik from 19th-century Borneo. *Below,* finger-woven motif of monkey and baby from present-day Guatemala. *Opposite,* monkeys and monkey-ghosts (?) on a slit-weave tapestry from the central coast of Peru, A.D. 1000–1500.

30

36

31

37

38

"Bats," *above*, on an unidentified Japanese textile. *Below*, detail of the lightning-striped unicorn from "The Pagan Paradise," *opposite*, a chenille-brocaded deep border woven in 17th-century Portugal or Andalusia.

40

BIRDS OF VARIED FEATHER. *Above*, cotton printed with swans, foliage, and pearls, from France, 1830–40. *Center*, the Ho-Ho bird, an adaptation of a resist-dyed cotton with handpainted areas in color from 19th-century Japan. *Opposite, corner*, "Bird of Paradise," a single motif from a hand-blocked English cotton of about 1830.

41

42

AUDUBON IN CHINA. *Above,* and *opposite,* four watercolors from a set of twelve painted on parchment after Audubon engravings by native artists under the direction of Jesuit missionaries in 19th-century China.

44

45

46

MADE IN FRANCE. *Above, left,* an example of the "pictures in silk" designed by
Philippe de Lasalle. *Right,* a 19th-century textile design showing how the diamond
shapes would interlock to make a repeat. *Below left,* a large square (scarf?) from
the famous silk city of Lyon, about 1960. *Opposite,* project for a wallpaper by an unknown designer, about 1770.

51

52

53

EAGLES ACROSS THE SEA. *Opposite, above,* project for a textile by J. B. Bony, "Napoleon's favorite designer," France, about 1805. *Opposite, below,* another project from the same period, showing Napoleon's initial and the crown he assumed. *Above,* part of a bandbox printed in the United States, 1800–10. The eagle has long been one of the world's most powerful symbols, Roman battalions using it on their battle standards.

54

55

MAN'S FOUR-FOOTED FRIENDS. *Above, top,* a lithograph by Karl F. T. Patsche, after Granville, France, about 1845. *Directly above,* roller-printed cotton from a sales-man's sample book, United States or England, second half of the 19th century. *Opposite,* section of a late 19th-century wallpaper featuring a reproduction of the painting *The Horse Fair* by Rosa Bonheur (1822–99).

42

57

58

BUTTERFLIES ARE BACK. *Above*, "Le Papillon," a wallcovering produced by Bob Mitchell, United States, 1971. *Below*, mammoth butterflies handprinted on velvet from a 1960s design for Ben Piazza by Harvey Smith. *Opposite*, roller-printed cotton, mid-19th-century England. See also pages 21 and 98 for ways this motif was used before giantism became fashionable, as it has in recent times.

44

60

"School of Fish," *above*, hanging of embroidered linen, Denmark, 1962. *Opposite, above*, "Insekten II," India ink drawing by Paul Flora of Austria, 1954. *Opposite, below*, a resist-dyed child's apron from early 20th-century China.

46

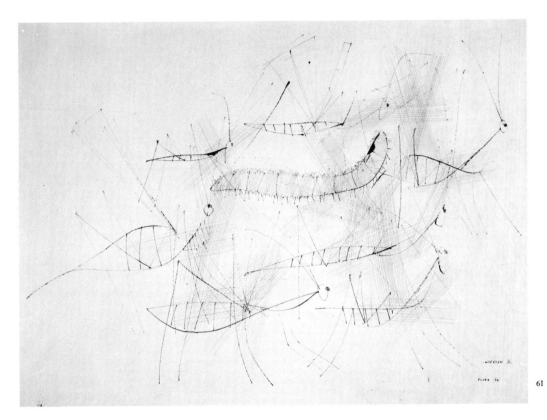

61

62

63

WONDERFULLY STRANGE. *Above,* an exemplary carpet of the "dragon," Sile, or "S" type for which the Dagestan district in the Caucasus was famous in the 16th and 17th centuries. It is especially interesting to note that all the large S shapes are filled in with small versions of the same motif, thus welding the composition. Collection of Doris Leslie Blau, New York. *Opposite,* an enigmatic device from one of the brocaded damasks treated in this section.

48

64

2 Enigmas

65

66

As this category did not exist it had to be invented. The data were plentiful enough; what was needed was a name. One by one a number of possibilities were discarded. "Abstractions" sounded fine until I realized that it could be applied to certain material in every category, and was, moreover, uncomfortably close to describing contemporary art in general. "Curiosities" and "Fantasies" likewise had to be rejected. Both labels might overlap other, firmly established classifications, or else would unduly limit the field. Frankly, "Enigmas" is not ideal, either. But some of its synonyms — "puzzling," "mysterious," "obscure" — suggest qualities that are inherent in pattern design and are treasured by those who practice it seriously. Virtuosity is their goal; if it can be reached without ostentation so much the better. A young designer of the present day, having executed what he feels is a genuine tour de force, might exclaim, "Is that out of sight!" If his appraisal is reasonably accurate, if he has avoided the common stereotypes and created something freshly strange, chances are the stockpile of world pattern has been enriched by another more-than-welcome enigma.

Not that determination always works. Flights of fancy are often unconscious; as free to others as to ourselves. Perhaps more free. On page 72 are a dozen curious shapes transcribed from Herbert Kuhn's *Rock Pictures of Europe*, a modest volume that deals principally with images found in Levantine Spain, near the Mediterranean, and thought to have been engraved and painted many centuries later than the larger, more naturalistic, "zoomorphic" pictures found in the caves of the final Ice Age farther north. From their truly enigmatic character Dr. Kuhn calls the cryptic images of the Spanish Levant "abstract," "cubist," and sometimes "demon" forms, suggesting that they denote "the transition from . . . hunting-magic to animism." That may be so. What I see in these silhouettes has infinitely greater implications: the effort to communicate ideas on the part of very primitive people who had no written language, nor were ever to have one. Yet they eschewed realism in order to express their fears — or whatever these shapes do express — in much the same manner that modern artists employ symbols. Were these prehistoric men living in Spain also "realists" at one time? One doesn't know, but it is thought that they might have been. The contemporary Spanish artist Joan Miró (b. 1893) gradually departed from the mannered realism he began his career with, and ultimately, in his paintings and ceramics, approximated his ancestors' rock pictures.

Miró is of course only one of many. There is not a single major abstractionist whose work was not representational at the start. This line of development

"Combed papers," *opposite*. A standard 1950s pattern of marbled bookpaper is inset with a more recent (1968) experiment, both examples having been produced by the firm of Douglas Cockerell and Son, Letchworth, England. This pigment-flotation technique is believed to have been devised in 16th-century Turkey, and thereafter was used persistently by the *dominotiers* of France (makers of playing cards, etc.), who also made the first sheets of patterned paper to decorate walls.

is so customary that we wonder whether it indicates the swinging of the pendulum of fashion from one extreme to the other, or whether stylization (as those who practice it would claim) signifies increased sensibility, not mere surfeit. In the case of the *t'ao-t'tieh* animal masks of China referred to in the previous section, either highly cultivated taste or strictly religious requirements must have occasioned their sophistication; it was not happenstance. Nor did these peculiar markings entirely disappear. Squared spirals find a place in Central American carvings and brickwork; in Caucasian rugs and woven "covers"; and, nearer our own time, the curved hook shapes on the appliquéd coats of the Ainu people on Japan's northern Hokkaido island strongly echo Shang-Yin bronzes.

Some of the tapestries of Peru's Tiahuanaco culture do more than merely echo the bronzes: an instance of what is known as "independent evolution" could equally well exemplify "diffusion." This, too, has been noted before. A major difference lies in the latitude a length of *cloth* offers. The shirts of wool tapestry worn by Tiahuanaco men of distinction — and preserved in dry, sandy burials, as in Egypt — are unique in textile design. If at first they suggest exceptionally elegant Cubism, patient study reveals an animal motif (presumably a puma or a jaguar) completely transformed into a variety of geometrical shapes that repeat themselves *while expanding and contracting according to the outlines of a pre-tailored garment.* It will be instantly appreciated that these particular Peruvian weavings could be classed under Animals or Geometrics, but I felt that their ambiguity qualified them as Enigmas.

Similar considerations prompted me to include the more flamboyant "paisley" patterns in this section: the big scrolls and arabesques that do not occur — either in the shawls woven at Kashmir, India, or, from French interpretations of the original Indian motifs, in the town of Paisley, Scotland — until the last half of the nineteenth century. While these terminate the evolution of the small, fat, lanceolate leaf first featured in Persian textiles, and surely owe a good deal to the tall, wind-tipped cyprus tree, their effect is scarcely Floral (or, strictly speaking, arboreal). John Irwin, Keeper of the Oriental Section at the Victoria & Albert Museum and the chief authority on India's painted cottons and woven shawls, has traced some of their motifs back to the crewel embroideries England sent to India, as models, from about the middle of the seventeenth century onward. Their intricate leaves and flowers evidently encouraged the native weavers in a tendency to embellishment they had already exhibited; soon every floral shape on the large cotton panels called *palampores* was filled with abstract "diapers." About a hundred and fifty years later, at the end of their own, somewhat longer period of popularity, the Kashmir/Paisley shawls were all interlocking ornament, with scant reference to nature. Mr. Irwin says that, woven on the new Jacquard looms in Scotland, they "could be bought for as little as £1, and the identical pattern printed on cotton cost a few shillings."

Another luxury product largely of oriental inspiration avoided being commercialized — as it has avoided being pinned down regarding its place of man-

ufacture. Vilhelm Slomann, the Danish art historian who gave the brocaded Bizarre Silks of the late seventeenth to early eighteenth century their name, was convinced that they were designed and woven somewhere in India, but few specialists agree with him. The provenance suggested ranges from France to Spain to Italy, and the picture is further confused by some of the more fabulous examples being found in Polish synagogues. What the genre reveals is how standard floral patterns, by a systematic emphasis on oddity, can become quite incomprehensible. "Chinoiserie" was never so outlandish, for the motifs of High Bizarre combine instruments of torture with monstrous vegetation, and — after a period lasting perhaps fifteen years — become normally floral again. Because of the exotic quality of the earlier Lucca patterns and the carnival spirit Venice was always famous for, a number of textile experts now attribute the more extreme Bizarre Silks to an unspecified source in northern Italy. Not until the height of Art Nouveau do we see anything comparably strange unless it is in the paintings of Hieronymus Bosch (1450–1516).

WHAT DOES IT REPRESENT? *Above,* a small rectangle of tapestry-woven wool and cotton from the Tiahuanaco period, Peru (7th–9th century A.D.). Instead of the fairly recognizable animal motifs on page 29, we seem to have plant forms here, and abstract shapes that could "mean" practically anything.

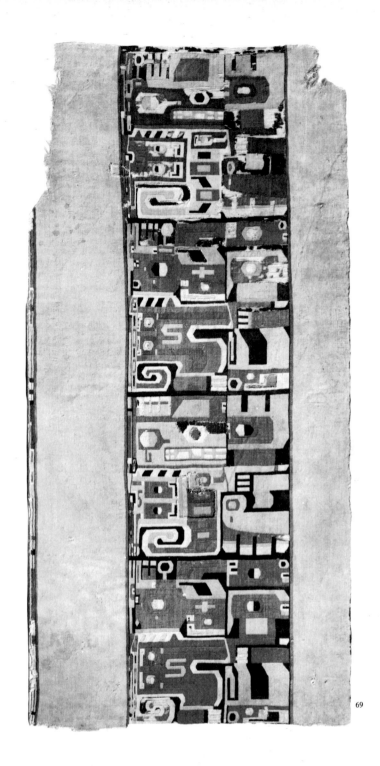

69

TRULY ENIGMATIC. *Opposite*, a dramatic example of the *t'ao-t-t'ieh* "gluttonous" mask on a bronze wine vessel from the Shang dynasty, China. On close study, protruding eyes, horns, and whiskers indicate various beasts, but the hooked shapes and square spirals are common to many cultures. *Above*, the motifs on this fragment of a tapestry shirt — again from Peru's versatile Tiahuanaco period — show the animal subject at its most abstract. Indeed, it could be a flat variation of the bronze *hu* opposite and suggests our own century's Cubism.

70

PATTERNED COSTUME. *Above center*, these halves of two dresses from 16th to 17th century Turkey must have belonged to rich children because the one on the left, using the "tiger stripe" motif, is described as being of silk and gold tissue; that on the right, with crescent shapes (and sun rays?) being of velvet. *Far right*, this appliquéd cotton coat from the northern Japanese island of Hokkaido is, on the other hand, an adult garment of great interest because, like all Ainu dress, it exhibits hook shapes or linear arabesques closely related to those of China and Peru.

71

72

73

74

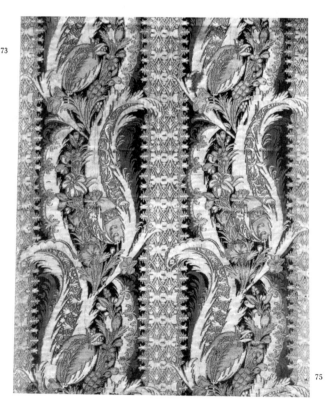

75

BIZARRE BEGINNINGS. *Above center*, the Desborough Mirror, a bronze from the British Iron Age, early 1st century A.D. *Above left*, a Moorish silk woven in late 14th- or early 15th-century Spain. *Above right*, a silk incorporating metal thread from early 18th-century Italy. The 1st-century mirror back amazingly anticipates late 19th-century Art Nouveau, while the Gothic freedom of the Spanish textile (in which giant "leaves" become wings), and the liberties taken with floral motifs in the Italian pattern — despite its strict symmetry — forecast the untrammeled invention that followed. *Opposite*, a brocaded damask shows the Bizarre era well under way.

58

BIZARRE TRIUMPHANT. *Above,* four inexplicable motifs from the so-called Bizarre Silks, of which the more extreme examples were doubtless made in or near Venice for a short period around the beginning of the 18th century. *Opposite,* a "turtle and pyramid" fragment exemplifying the style at its oddest. Should one say the style disappeared or that it was absorbed? Inevitably, the exotic becomes domesticated.

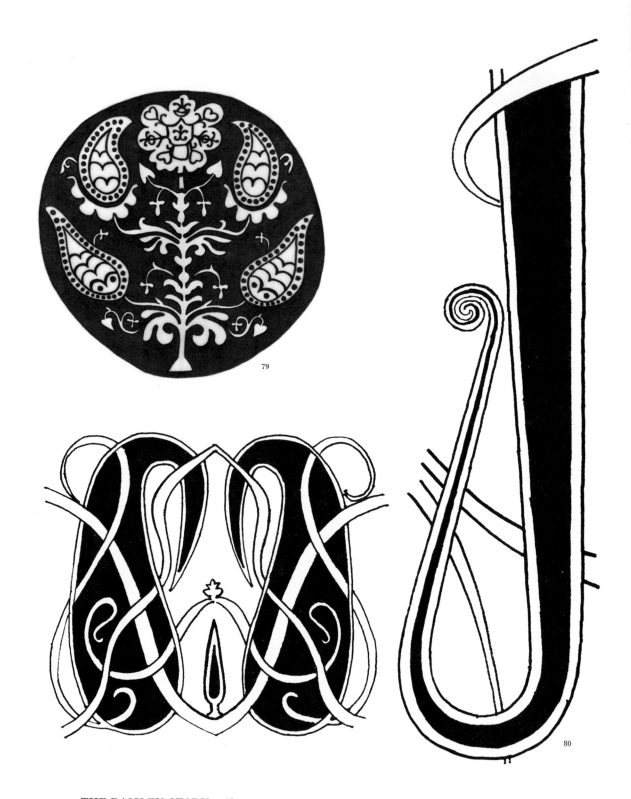

THE PAISLEY STORY. *Above, top,* a drawing of a plant motif from 6th- or 7th-century Egypt shows that the bent leaf we call the paisley cone flourished a thousand years before it was popularized by the Kashmir shawl. *Directly above,* arabesques and scrolls typical of the mounting extravagance in late 19th-century design. *Opposite,* one corner of a handsome but modest shawl embroidered in India on plain twill wool.

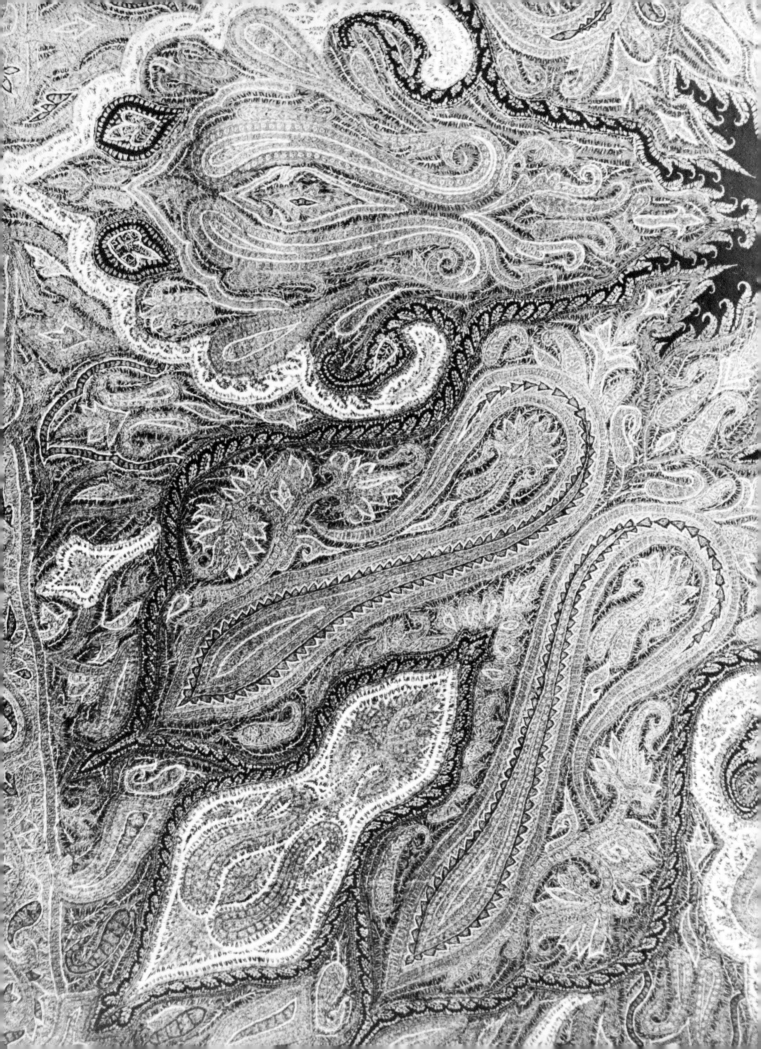

82

84

86

ALL ARE CALLED PAISLEY. *Opposite, upper left,* working sketch for French "paisley" made around 1900. *Opposite, upper right,* part of a large-scale pattern produced both as wallpaper and companion fabric by Woodson Taulbee in New York in the middle 1950s. *Opposite, lower left,* a late 19th-century French wallpaper imported to the United States by A. L. Diamant. *Opposite, lower right,* an 18th-century French fabric from the "Jacques Martin scrapbook," gift of Josephine Howell to the Cooper-Hewitt Museum of Design — a type of repeat that has inspired endless imitation patchwork. (See also the more regularly imbricated pattern on page 11.) This, and many "paisleys" could more accurately be referred to as "Indienne," and it is ironic that none of these four patterns were made at Paisley, Scotland. *Above,* one end of a long mid-19th-century shawl executed in India from a European (probably French) design.

87

"Girls drinking a toast," *above*, a 13th- or 14th-century Hispano-Moresque slit tapestry which reveals that not only animals were enclosed by frames far into the Middle Ages. To compare sophistication in garment patterns see also page 137: a dossal embroidered in Germany at the same period. *Opposite*, "The Umbrella," a chalk drawing from the 1940s by renowned poster artist E. McKnight Kauffer, here converted to line.

88

3 Figures

Human faces and figures have been as scarce in the decorative arts, as a whole, as they have been plentiful in painting and sculpture. True, the amulet-size "Venuses" are more artifact than art, and the stick figures in cave paintings betray a total lack of interest in figure representation, but the running, leaping warriors of the "Second Hunters' Style" referred to above express bodily grace and movement with a directness that anticipates Matisse (1869–1954) in his *Jazz* series of cut papers, and this around 10,000 B.C. Some seven thousand years later, when people reappear in art, starting a long procession that begins with cylindrical seals and the stately friezes at Sumer, they are more realistic and more rigid. These qualities produce an art generally described as "hier-archic," in which the statues look straight ahead and the pictures show figures and objects in profile. Egypt made the most of these limitations. Frontalism was felt to be a dignified way to present rulers and important persons sculp-turally, while the profiling not only solved many problems of representation and expediency in carved and painted bas-relief, it facilitated a less formal type of picture: the "journeyman" painting found in Middle and New Kingdom tombs, of about 2100–1400 B.C. At once sharply observed and poetic, these casual-seeming vignettes, beautifully presented in *Egyptian Painting* (Skira, 1954), constituted a precious legacy.

But where were the heirs? Here again the native Copts appear singularly obtuse. Just as they ignored their forebears' mastery of the repeat, they chose to base the style of their little woven pictures on the widespread Hellenism of the early Christian era, merely adding square halos for the living, round ones for the dead. Greece itself had pursued a separate course. The flat "plank" amu-lets from the Cyclades Islands, the bands of figures on the huge sacrificial vases from the eighth century B.C. cemetery at Dipylon, are enchantingly "stylish" but exceedingly primitive: they owe nothing to the Near East or to Egypt. Within a few centuries, however — by the middle of the fifth — the Greeks had freed the human image from both the silhouette and frontalism, without doubt because of seeing nude bodies in daily exercise and athletic contests; half a dozen known sculptors and vase painters reached a height of refinement in depicting the human body never attained before or since. Unfortunately, many of the vases are overwhelmed by large ungainly palmettes that were clearly added to the figured design, after it had been painted, by an assistant who had the well-known horror of a vacuum, if his master did not. To put it boldly, the Greeks, for all of their manual skill and epicureanism, were curiously lacking in the visual restraint we call good taste. Their public buildings, though of marble, were brightly painted, and while their garments contributed fluidity to sculpture

"Man with Pheasant," *opposite*, a late 18th- or early 19th-century cotton blockprinted in polychrome, its provenance "probably Spain." This is our first exposure to explicit *chinoiserie*, although oriental elements entered into many of the textiles woven in 14th-century Lucca (pages 26 and 27), as well as into the Bizarre Silks in the foregoing section on Enigmas.

(especially when wetness was simulated), all those folds of cloth must have been, in reality, rather dowdy. They were wise to exalt the nude.

It is interesting that this aspect of Greek art was rarely disseminated by Hellenism. We understand that the Romans, for example, were shocked by Greek nudity, and it goes without saying that by the time they had adopted the Christian religion — which is essentially Jewish and puritanical — bodies were well covered, as they are in the Byzantine mosaics at Ravenna. Iconoclasm, in fact, springs from questions of taste. Roman art is almost epitomized by ultra-realistic portrait sculpture, and the New Rome at Constantinople is said to have been a city of statues. These obviously could have been an embarrassment to the new religion and could have led to the first brief span of "idol-breaking" in the fourth century, and to the prolonged controversy over the use of images during the eighth and ninth. As noted, human subject matter dominated the small tapestries the Coptic Egyptians (and the Syrians) made to ornament their tunics, but after the Second Council of Nicaea in 787, the Church can be said to have appropriated the human figure for its own circumspect use.

This continued to be true throughout the western Middle Ages: the proverbial Age of Faith. Sacred persons became the focal points on ecclesiastical vestments, in mosaics covering entire apses, and on the exteriors of cathedrals and throughout their stained-glass windows. What are known as Books of Hours also contained figures, not always in a religious context. The Duc de Berry's famous volume of devotions illuminated by the Limbourg brothers (in 1413–1416) emphasizes the months of the year rather than the canonical hours and is both a reflection of the "new" art of landscape painting and a miniature counterpart to the worldly, often allegorical tapestries that were beginning to be woven to flatter the nobility and to keep their castles warm. The tapestries on pages 137 and 196 show the contrast between a religious and a secular subject, the patterning in each being a striking clue to its period.

Outside Europe the question of the religious significance of a pattern or a motif usually requires an answer from a specialist. All that I can vouchsafe is that the Paracas Necropolis culture of Peru, dating from the first century A.D., and the final Tiahuanaco culture (which preceded the Inca civilization that Pizarro destroyed virtually overnight, in 1532) used human figures with equal flair, and very differently. Yet their fantasy is such that either superstition — or considerable humor! — is involved. If these apparitions and acrobats were to emerge during our own era we would list them as Novelties without hesitation: motifs suitable for children (e.g., on the poncho-shirt, page 76) or for childish adults. Because that, alas, is what patterned figure subjects have currently come to. When Andy Warhol repeats a silk-screened head of Marilyn Monroe thirty times over, under the impression that he is satirizing wallpaper, he is exhibiting his ignorance of the nature of pattern. In fairness to those rare designers who have attempted to use human faces or figures in subtle repeat, it

70

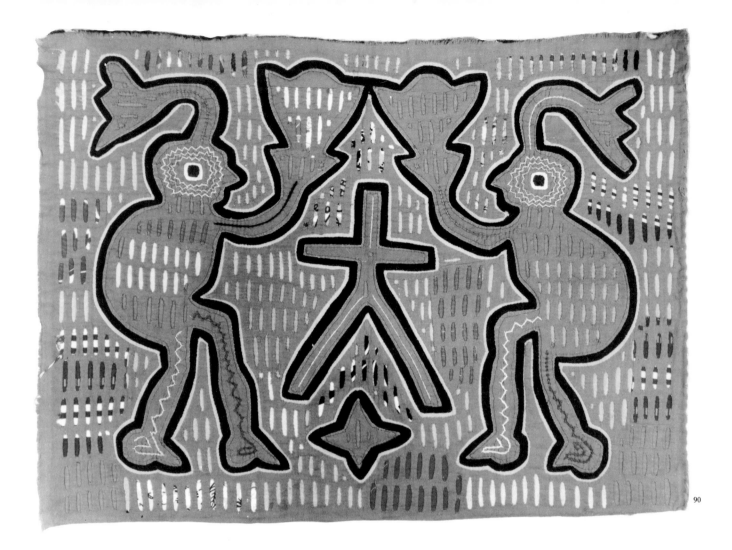

90

must be said that they have centuries of proscription, of iconoclasm, working against them.

The single exception seems to be figures that occur in landscapes. These appear so frequently in the satins and velvets of the Safavid Dynasty in sixteenth- and seventeenth-century Persia that one wonders how such textiles were used. For garments? For backgrounds? From the small fragments that exist it is plausible to think of the material — which is yardage — as couch or cushion covering. But a piece of "Hunting Scene" polychrome velvet in the Boston Museum of Fine Arts is described as having been part of "the ceiling of a tent," which suggests almost unimaginable grandeur. In a later section, devoted to Scenics, we hazard a guess that these Persian textiles were the prototypes for the cotton prints called *toiles de Jouy*, and in the more modest landscapes of the *toile* patterns human figures become incidental. This is in line with present-day prejudices, and our feeling as to what is or is not appropriate for apparel or for decorating fabrics. Taking a cue from animal subjects, it would appear that figures, too, are acceptable to the degree they are impersonal.

PATCHWORK REVERSED. *Above*, a 20th-century cotton "mola" from the San Blas Islands, Panama. The technique of cutting away layers of cloth — instead of adding them — may not have originated with the native women of these equatorial islands, but they made it into a unique, highly colorful art form. Until recently each design was a personal expression, and the maker wore it proudly in the opening of her blouse.

91

DRAWING THE HUMAN FIGURE. *Above*, reading from top left to bottom right, notice that these figures found in southern Europe and northern Africa become less and less realistic, with the exception of the outlined forms described as "demons." *Opposite, above*, a variety of figures from different registers — or horizontal bands — on an 8th-century B.C. burial jar found in the Dipylon cemetery near Athens and now in the Metropolitan Museum. *Opposite, below*, Greek vase motif of a satyr and nymph which is delightful in spite of the competition from oversize, badly placed palmettes.

92

93

94

95

74

96

9

HELLENISM. *Opposite, above,* a 5th-century A.D. Coptic tapestry, "undoubtedly used as a funeral hanging," and quite likely depicting the four Evangelists against an all-over pattern of heads and confronted birds whose significance ("souls"?) is unknown. *Opposite, below,* detail of the same hanging. *Center,* male figure from an "Eastern Mediterranean" unidentified tapestry. *Above,* "A Woman's Head" from "Syria or Egypt, 3rd or 4th century, possibly earlier." The spread of classical culture and motifs — of Hellenism — was patently erratic and depended on trade centers. Observe the guilloche in the column separating the youth from the striped curtain.

THOSE PERUVIANS! *Above*, a child's poncho-shirt of wool embroidered in cotton from the Paracas Necropolis Culture on the south coast, about A.D. 100. *Center*, the detail of what is called "a falling or dancing figure" (!) from the same garment. *Opposite*, acrobats or reflected figures from the Tiahuanaco culture some six hundred years later, exploiting the design device known as Counterchange. Whether or not the Peruvians sought humor, they often attained it — along with nearly every weaving technique any people have ever practiced.

76

102

103

THOSE PERSIANS! *Opposite*, a prisoner being led through woods in what could also be called a Scenic subject of "probably the 17th century." *Above left*, a detail of a late 16th-century miniature of girls bathing known as "The Eavesdropper." *Above right*, the turbaned figure with a wine bottle is from the esteemed Safavid Dynasty during the reign of Shah Abbas (1589–1628). Any artistic convention that emphasizes flat surfaces greatly aids pattern design.

A New Book of
CHINESE ORNAMENTS
Invented & Engraved by I. Pillement

MASTER OF CHINOISERIE. *Opposite*, the title page of one of several books on ornament by Jean-Baptiste Pillement. *Above left*, an engraving from "Petits Parasols Chinois."
Above right, an engraving from a series called "The Months." Pillement was as eclectic
as he was exotic, supplementing his slight knowledge of the Orient with Rococo scrollwork, tropical vegetation, and romantic rusticity. See also the Scenic pattern on page 168.

107

CLASSICAL THEMES IN TOILES DE JOUY. *Above,* cameolike medallions on a dia-
mond-diapered background, printed by copperplate and dated 1817. *Opposite,* "Leda
and the Swan," another copperplate print designed about 1798 by J. B. Huet for the same
Oberkampf factory at Jouy, France. While both patterns were inspired by the rediscovery of Pompeii and Herculaneum in 1748 (and neither is a typical landscape "toile"),
the Leda-Swan subject is unequaled in the way it integrates a number of lovely shapes
with an ingenuity any designer might envy. For stylistic contrast see also pages 136
and 160.

109

110

FIGURES AND FACES. *Above, top,* a blockprinted cotton (of a man sowing?) from Alsace, France, 1825. *Directly above,* an 1893 English nursery wallpaper taken from Almanac drawings by Kate Greenway (1846–1901). *Opposite,* machine-printed wallpaper designed by Charles Dana Gibson for M. H. Birge and Sons, United States, 1902.

84

112

113

THE SILHOUETTE. *Above, top,* the most famous Kamares vessel with its Minoan sea motifs, about 1750 B.C. *Directly above,* "Portraits of the Clinton Family," United States, 1839, by Fidèle Edourt (1789–1861). *Opposite,* some figures and philodendron leaves adapted from Henri Matisse's book on cut papers entitled *Jazz,* which E. Tériade first published in 1947. Although such shapes were not given a name until the strict economic policies of the financier Etienne de Silhouette (1707–67) inspired it, they have been a prime form of expression from the earliest times, and at present are deemed admirable not for their fidelity, but insofar as they combine observation and freedom.

114

115

"Serpentine Roses," *above*, described as "a wall hanging stencilled and painted on canvas," has a frieze of carnations (not shown), probably from France, 1775–90. *Opposite*, an adaptation from an 1830 textile design "in the manner of J. B. Bony" — about whom see caption page 41. The roses are notable for the even distribution of flowers on their meandering growth lines, and the single motif, opposite, is a striking example of the in-filling of fairly realistic outlines with unrelated geometrical diapers.

116

4 Florals

117

Assuming that patterns had their beginnings in primitive "industry," and that, due to the rigors of the repeat, all patterns are basically geometrical, the first craftsmen to design directly from nature were creative in every sense of the word. They might have lived in Crete. The Minoan civilization was one of the world's oldest (at its height around 1600 B.C.), and the freedom it displayed in its sea-inspired motifs gives us, in effect, a foretaste of Art Nouveau and the free-forms of Hans (later Jean) Arp (1887–1966) and scores of other contemporary artists. Yet for an unknown reason Minoan culture — named for the legendary King Minos, of the labyrinth and its bull-like minotaur to whom Greek youths and maidens were sacrificed — flourished for only a few centuries and then disappeared. When Crete was heard from again, shortly before the Christian era, it was as a small maritime nation harboring pirates.

Another equally possible instigator of naturalism was Egypt. Wilfred Blunt, in giving a detailed account of the Herbal in *The Art of Botanical Illustrations*, states, "Curiosity regarding the medicinal properties of plants was the humble origin of scientific botany," and refers to "a small roofless hall at the eastern end of the Great Temple of Thutmose III at Karnak" as being "the earliest florilegium known to us." Carved in limestone, the Karnak bas-reliefs date from the fifteenth century B.C. and record some two hundred and seventy-five plants that the victorious pharaoh brought back from a Syrian campaign. At the time these semi-naturalistic shapes (some of which, according to George Schweinfurth, the authority on Egyptian flora, were imaginary) must have seemed a marvelous departure from the stylized forms of the papyrus on the capitals of the surrounding columns. They may well have been added to the repertoire of plant motifs that Egypt so skillfully made abstract.

One of the most obsessed Egyptologists was William H. Goodyear, an American. In his *The Grammar of the Lotus*, published in 1891, he blithely saw "not the rose-washed bloom we call the lotus," but the blue or white *nymphaeas* — "a large water-lily whose leaves lie close to the water" — as the inspiration not only for Egypt's lotiform and other columns (scornfully dismissing the papyrus) but for the majority of Greek motifs as well: their Ionic columns having capitals of lily petals bent backward, the palmettes and anthemions on their vases being lilies seen in profile, and the universal rosette a wide-open lily viewed from above! Nor did he stop there. The French *rinceau*, or foliated scroll, was derived — for Mr. Goodyear — from the curving stems of the flower when they were pulled from the water, and the egg-and-dart motif was simply a row of unopened buds. As for the vine: most vine leaves were partial (or partly submerged) lily pads . . . all of this ignoring the fact that the art of Egypt used a number of plant motifs besides the lily/lotus, each of them suitable for artistic propagation.

Actually, as we have observed before, other cultures seem to have been largely unaware of, or indifferent to, Egyptian prototypes. Compared with the

CHASUBLE. *Opposite,* a brocaded vestment from 19th-century France with a symmetrical dignity that suggests the material was designed for its ecclesiastical purpose rather than having been made (as so many vestments were) from cast-off court costumes.

motifs of Greece and Persia, those of Egypt did not "travel" well. While the lotus cult still has its adherents, nothing in the history of design has the persistence of the acanthus, with the "Tree of Life" and the "pomegranate" offering some rivalry, although these are labels of convenience and the motifs themselves lack definition. To take the older term first, there does appear to have been a sacred tree design in the art of the Mesopotamian and Asiatic peoples, but its form varied widely with each, and sometimes was no more than a leafy stick. For religious purposes, no more would be necessary. Our only interest in the "tree," however named, lies in its compositional value, for it initially separated human or animal figures (as in the seals of Sumer and Nineveh), and later supported a wealth of embellished flowers — which have been called "beefsteak blossoms" — on the cotton hangings painted in late medieval India. "Pomegranate" patterning was a similar aid to composition. Adèle Weibel's outline of its evolution, given on page 92, is far too inclusive for my taste, but there can be no doubt that it was the result of a long-term synthesis. This gave (and still gives) Renaissance "pomegranates" an indeterminate character that assured their popularity, especially in self-toned damask. (Few people tire of the nearly invisible.) An extraordinary aspect of Renaissance thought was its obliviousness to nature, in spite of Petrarch's climbing a mountain, and Leonardo's and a few others' lovely drawings of plants. Jacopo Bellini, Pisanello, and Pollaiuolo are among the artists known to have designed patterns for their paintings, but only Botticelli seems to have picked real flowers to scatter on his subjects' dresses.

Then fashion changed. If at most times floral subjects are in a process of transition, they were disconcertingly so during the seventeenth and eighteenth centuries. Accepting all the stylistic and technical complexities of the period, Peter Thornton's book *Baroque and Rococo Silks* manages to give a graph of the trends toward and away from "naturalism." Oriental influences are taken into account, as is Bizarre fantasy, but it is evident that Mr. Thornton particularly admires the kind of realism Jean Revel (b. 1684) — "in his own time the most famous of all the great designers at Lyons" — achieved with a system of shading colored threads into each other that is called *pointes rentrés*. A bit later "pictures in silk" reached their zenith (some would say nadir) in the designs of Philippe de Lasalle (1723–1803), whose career began in the 1750s and came to a sudden close with the outbreak of the French Revolution. Subsequent to that momentous event, there was a token emphasis on simplicity, and on cotton or "voile," though Napoleon's own love of the grandiose soon returned official taste to a silken standard. Meanwhile, under the laurel wreaths that were a hallmark of neoclassicism and the Directoire, the bucolic world of *toiles de Jouy* flourished.

But, for the West by and large, the center of creative design had moved north. Robert Schmutzler in his encyclopedic volume *Art Nouveau* writes, "The visionary painter-poet William Blake (1757–1827) . . . anticipated the leitmotiv of

Art Nouveau completely. . . . There is not a single feature in his work that does not bear the sign of exaggeration . . . ruled by a strange elegance and an instinct that delights in ornament and decoration." After a long exposure to the popular art of India, England embraced *chinoiserie* without reservation, combining it with her love of gardens. This was a heady mixture. It led to the unabashed exoticism of the Prince Regent's Royal Pavilion at Brighton, and thence to the excesses of the "art manufactures" of the Great Exhibition of 1851 in what became known as the Crystal Palace. William Morris (1834–1896) reacted to this visual medley by proposing his own interpretation of medievalism. When the Pre-Raphaelite movement — which gave Morris his chief moral support — in due time merged with international Art Nouveau, the wide array of floral forms does not need to be imagined; it still surrounds us. For the past century, up until the past few years, two out of three patterns could be described as Floral.

VICTORIAN VALANCE. *Above*, calla lilies executed in gros point in wool on canvas, mid-19th century, England. The technique was often called "Berlin work."

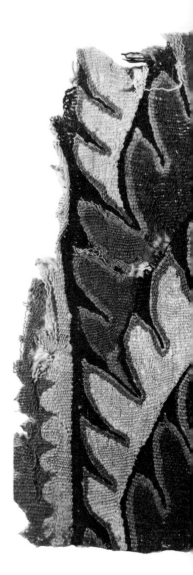

119

EARLY LEAVES AND FRUIT. *Far left*, an interpretation of a linen and wool tapestry curtain border from 3rd- or 4th-century Egypt. *Center*, fragment of a similar nature from the 5th or 6th century. *Above*, what may be the earliest and most realistic extant representation of the pomegranate — also from Coptic Egypt. For more of the "pomegranate" story, in pictures, see pages 106 and 107.

122

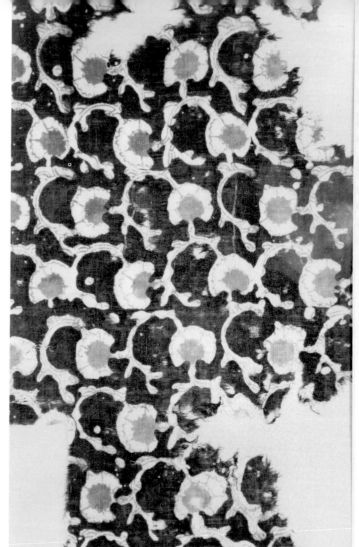

96

125

126

INTRODUCING INDIA. *Opposite, above left,* cotton printed in 12th- or 13th-century India but found at Fostat, Egypt. *Opposite, above right,* another cotton originating from 14th- to 16th-century India and found at Fostat. *Opposite, below,* portion of a wool shawl from "Persia or North India, 18th century." The resist-dyed cottons could have survived only in warm dry Egyptian sand, and doubt about the provenance of the shawl may be due to the mixture of Persian spacing and Indian profusion. *Above left,* impression from a printer's block of 19th-century India, and, *right,* a continuous pattern with a half-drop match the author made from it for self-toned flocking.

127

128

WHAT MAKES A PATTERN PERSIAN? *Top,* a drawing of the most typical Persian patterning one might find, with rows of plants and butterflies alternately turning to either side. *Above left,* a brocaded and stamped plain cloth from 17th-century Persia. *Above right,* an ornately brocaded compound cloth from the same period. *Opposite,* a definitive prayer rug of the "vase" type in the collection of Joseph V. McMullan, with its mihrab arch which, five times a day, would be turned toward Mecca.

130

131

132

TURKISH DELIGHTS. *Above left*, the single blossom of a 16th-century textile from Turkey, "in-filled" with various floral motifs, and *above right*, similarly stylized tulips on undulating growth lines. *Opposite, above*, a pattern of staggered leaves enriched with hyacinths along their veins. *Opposite, below*, the author's version of a standard Turkish carnation pattern that was produced as a wallcovering in two sizes, meant to supplement each other by creating illusory distance, as in a hallway or alcove. Original pieces of the serpentine tulips and the zigzag leaves are in the Museum of Fine Arts, Boston, and the Metropolitan Museum respectively.

100

133

134

101

135

136

137

138

THE TREE OF LIFE, SO CALLED. *Opposite, above*, part of a crewel-embroidered curtain from 17th-century England. *Opposite, below*, section of painted and dyed cotton from 17th- or 18th-century India. *Above, top*, simplified drawing of a painted and dyed *palampore*, or bedspread, made on the northern Coromandel Coast, after a plate in John Irwin and Katharine B. Brett's *Origins of Chintz*. *Directly above*, a panel of 17th-century English crewelwork featuring a "Chinese" rockery, the base of so much Indian "Tree of Life" merchandise made for the various East India Companies.

103

139

ACANTHUS AND PALMETTE. *Above left*, a silk and linen brocatelle from 15th- or 16th-century Italy that can instructively be contrasted — as regards style — with the Coptic acanthus leaves on pages 94–95. *Center*, detail of a tunicle brocaded with gold palmettes in early 16th-century Venice. *Opposite, above*, the author's revision of the same pattern from a diagonal to a serpentine stripe at the request of a stylist in the textile industry who feared any repeat that "leaned." *Opposite, below*, a lion composed of acanthus leaves in a German engraving of the 17th century.

140

141

142

105

143

147

148

PICK YOUR POMEGRANATE. *Opposite, above left,* the accepted reconstruction of the earliest known fragment of European wallpaper, found at Christ's College, Cambridge, in 1509. *Beside it, right,* unusually realistic pomegranates from the late 16th century, Italy. *Opposite, below left,* damask, "probably Spanish, end of the 16th century." *Beside it, right,* almost certainly the handsomest of the pomegranate/palmette/pine cone patterns, a woven silk from 16th-century Italy. *Above, left,* detail of an altar frontal from late 15th-century Florence. *Below right,* a *ferronerie,* or "ironwork," variation of the same pattern group, this example preceding the others by approximately a century: a case of abstraction-before-naturalism.

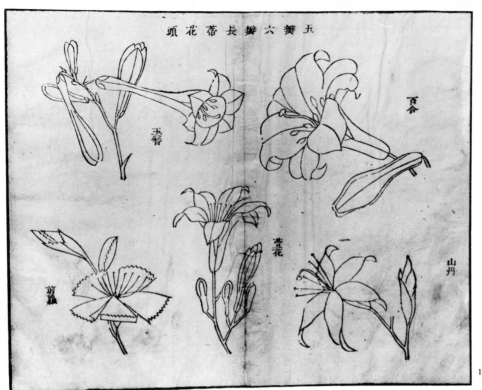

149

150

A LYRICAL INTERLUDE. *Above,* folded page from *The Mustard Seed Garden,* the principal drawing manual of 17th-century China, here depicting "tuberose and related flowers." *Below,* "Ferns," sketch from a woven border by an unknown French artist, 1805–15. *Opposite, above,* another textile design from France, 1785–1800. *Opposite, below,* white taffeta skirt length brocaded in colors from the celebrated factory at Spitalfields, England, which, producing its own brand of romanticism, flourished during the mid–18th century.

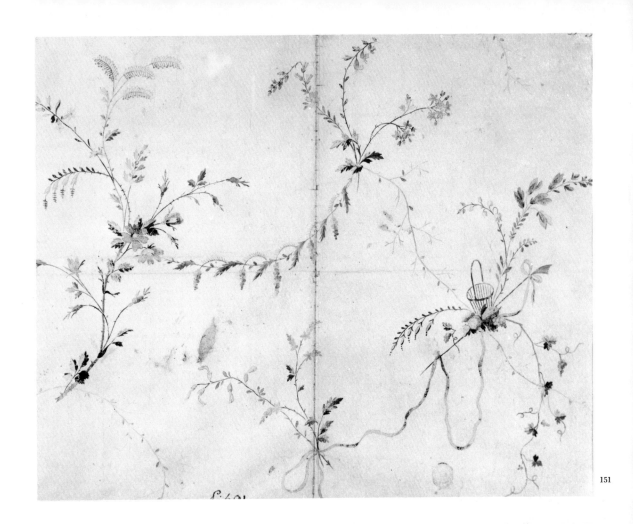

151

152

153

110

154

155

THE GOTHIC REVIVAL. *Opposite, far left*, a flocked wallpaper embodying the "Tudor rose," designed by Augustus Welby Pugin (1812–52) for the houses of Parliament. *Center*, another pseudo-Gothic paper — using imbricated arches — commissioned for that fantastic pastiche, the Royal Pavilion at Brighton. *Above right*, a palmette pattern by Owen Jones (1809–74), whose monumental *The Grammar of Ornament* commemorated the Great Exhibition at "the Crystal Palace" in 1851. Sponsored by Prince Albert, the huge display was intended to improve public taste, whereas in fact it may merely have emulsified it.

156

MR. MORRIS PROTESTS. *Above left,* a pattern such as this represented all that initially offended William Morris. *Center,* Morris's own pattern "Willow" is the designer at his simple best, while "Single Stem," *opposite, far right,* by his pupil and successor J. H. Dearle, marks the work of Morris and Co. at its most worldly. Seeking to rectify the design situation in Victorian England, Morris's return to nature was intermittent, his medievalism largely rhetorical. The most accomplished designer since Pillement, he ran the gamut from neo-Classicism to a Baroque flamboyance that prefigured the Art Nouveau whose "decadence" he abhorred.

112

157

158

113

159

160

ART NOUVEAU. *Above, top,* a free interpretation of Hermann Obrist's 1895 "whip-lash" wall hanging entitled "Cyclamen" (from Robert Schmutzler's *Art Nouveau*); *directly above,* a line drawing of Charles Annesley Voysey's 1896 wallpaper "Tulip and Bird" from the same volume. Together, these could represent the extremes of the first style of international importance since the Renaissance. Art Nouveau embraced many elements, from the scrollwork on the Desborough Mirror (page 58), to the rococo *chinoiserie* in the Royal Pavilion (page 165), Voysey's symmetry being atypical. *Opposite,* a panel of silk, chiffon, and net embroidered between 1900 and 1910 after a design by Hector Guimard (1867–1942) — famous for the Paris Métro entrances — which represents the style at its purest.

114

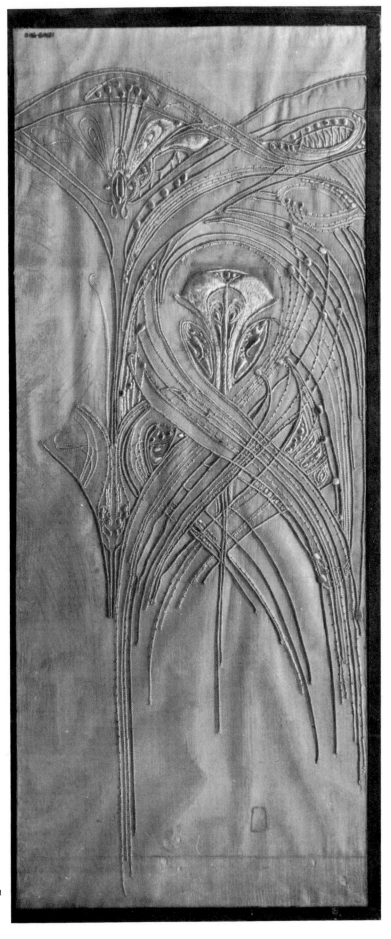

161

MODERNE/DECO. *Opposite*, a textile of appliquéd materials from "Paris or Munich, about 1925." *Above, top*, detail of a batik velvet stole worked with jet beads, France, 1915–20. *Above left*, wallpaper designed by R. Crevel and printed from woodblocks, France, 1920. *Above right*, printed cotton designed by Raoul Dufy (1877–1955), France, 1930. Cubism had developed as Art Nouveau declined, and the decorative style that became applied Cubism (especially at the German art school known as the Bauhaus, 1919–35) was first called Arte Moderne, more recently Art Deco. The illustration opposite is curiously reminiscent of some Bizarre Silks, while the Dufy pattern — consciously or not — has a secondary motif strictly in line with the 17th- and 18th-century textiles that used damask grounds for their brocading.

166

167

168

A PERSONAL MISCELLANY. *Opposite, above,* "Marguerites," one of the author's more successful wallpapers, about 1939, first printed by hand, then by machine. *Opposite, below,* "Giant Bamboo," a 1954 stripe in which a score of "bamboo" patterns reached their culmination, here printed on thin sheets of cork for a foyer. *Above,* "Field of Grass," 1968, a 15-foot-high, 40-foot-long mosaic wall prepared by the author and his wife by the traditional "reverse" method of gluing many shades of green Italian glass *tesserae* to sheets of paper that were "flipped" into wet cement and later soaked off. Commissioned by Eleanor Le Maire Associates for the Commerce Towers Building at Kansas City, Missouri.

"The Swastika in China," *above*, embroidered silk sleeves from the 19th century. *Opposite page*, "Black Sun," an exercise by a student at the Cooper Union School of Art and Engineering, New York. Many centuries before the Nazis appropriated it as "their" symbol, the swastika had evolved from cross-banded fretwork in every great culture East and West, this particular pattern being of interest for the use it also makes of squared hooks and the device of Counterchange. The illusion on the opposite page is equally notable because it is composed of sticks of equal length.

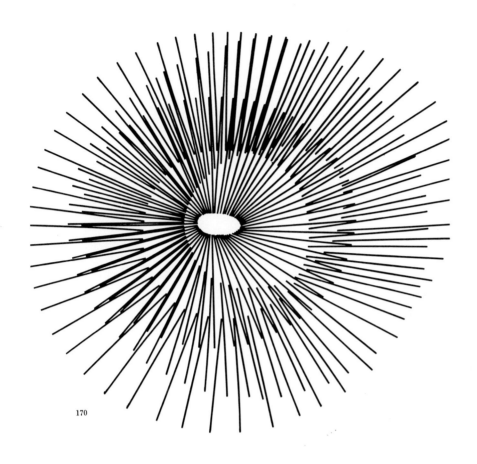

170

5 Geometrics

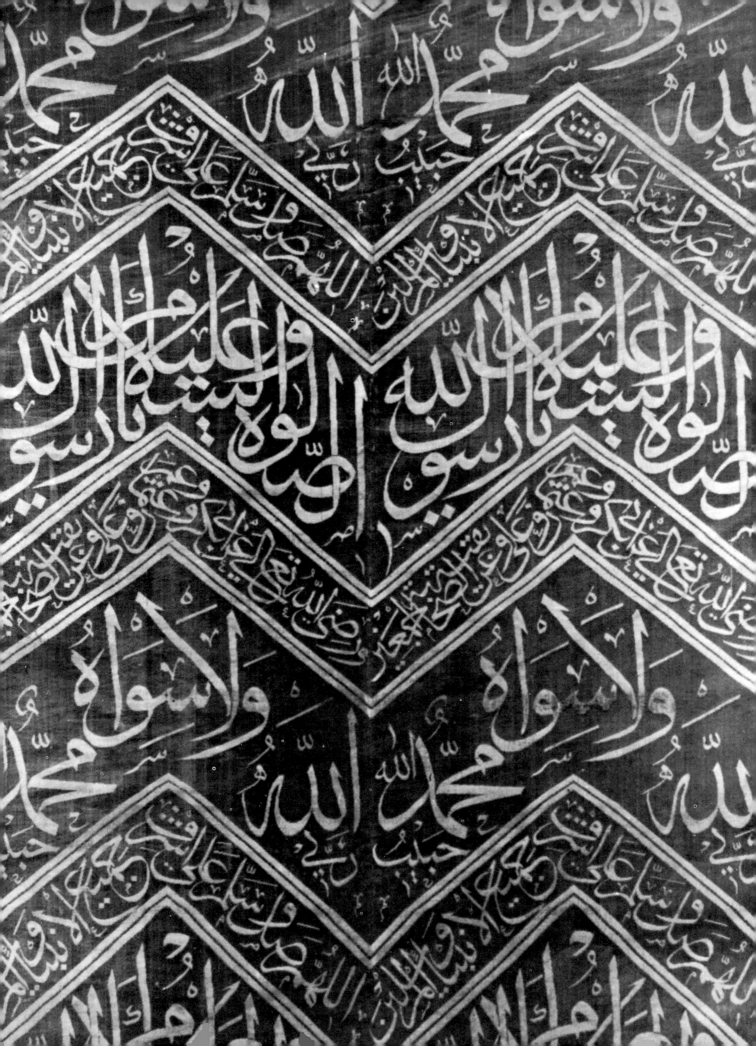

Not without irony, an increasing number of contemporary patterns fall into the same category — Geometrics — as those that were made six thousand years ago at the edge of recorded history. In some respects design is back where it started. Designers easily enough approximate the shards that gather dust in the basements of scores of museums, but a deep spiral border, say, on a whole piece of pottery from the Neolithic or New Stone Age of China is hard to equal; a wall decoration even harder. In the Metropolitan Museum of Art there is an all-over pattern of turquoise-blue glazed tile that perfectly substantiates the "art in industry" theory. It is from Djoser's reign during Dynasty III of Egypt (2667–2648 B.C.) and obviously a translation into a more precious and lasting material of the rush-mat motif typical of extremely ancient times, when the Egyptians buried the dead in square pits lined, as were their homes, with mats. Another, still more architectural pattern is in the British Museum: part of an engaged column found at Urak, the biblical Erech. This shows how Sumerian builders at about 4000 B.C. sought to relieve the heavy effect of unfired clay walls by pressing zigzag or "herringbone" bands of small multicolor terracotta cones into them. We cannot know how frequently in remote times walls and floors were ornamented, but it is safe to guess that not a few mosaic borders and painted panels — in the civilizations that followed these — were intended to create a certain atmosphere (like the tile "matting") or to improve an architectural shortcoming (like the variegated chevrons).

Geometrical motifs excel for both purposes. Although Roman pavements have been referred to in Part I, the Roman villas at Pompeii and Herculaneum provide the first explicit exercises in interior design (not mere arrangement) that I know of. Given the opportunity, in books or at the site, we should look at the four decorative styles — ranging from the second through the first century B.C. and named "Encrusted," "Architectural," "Ornate," and "Intricate" — less for their textured or scenic subject matter than for their attempt to impose proportion and perspective on walls that were quite ordinarily flat. It is a problem in creating space that in our own century was to engross Piet Mondrian, having already occupied his countrymen Jan Vermeer and Pieter de Hooch, among others. A discussion of the special relationships obtainable by employing the Golden Section (or Mean) or Dynamic Symmetry would lead too far astray, but, in speaking of geometry, it is well to keep in mind that not only "Euclid alone has looked on Beauty bare"; every architect and designer worth his salt has done so. And, in varying degrees, every painter of stature. In the western masterworks of the past no one needs a diagram to realize that a firm construction underlies the pictorial elements. Indeed, modern art, beginning with Cézanne's watercolors, is inclined to make a picture consist primarily of its

ISLAM REMEMBERS. *Opposite*, a silk tomb cover from 16th- or 17th-century Turkey, with inscriptions from the Koran. At least two popular types of design are incorporated here: "herringbone" stripes on a large scale, and elegant calligraphy.

structure. For a purist, contemporary sculpture is to be preferred over painting: its planes and forms are actual rather than simulated.

Calligraphy, too, can be pure geometry, and perhaps all the more esthetically enjoyable if one cannot read it. Whereas printing also depends on qualities of line and on spacing, only in handwritten script and notably in the styles of writing that have been developed in the Near and Far East do we find the controlled flair ("flourishing" was the American word for fancy penmanship) that makes calligraphy a fine art. The "demon" rock pictures of the Spanish Levant were apparently an effort to communicate with pictographs. They may have failed because it was too early, because there wasn't enough urgent information. At Sumer, when trade demanded it, signs became syllables, and, among the Phoenicians, an alphabet. Early China did not have one, but her ideograms gave rise to brush-painting. Throughout the Orient — it scarcely needs to be said — the brushstroke was exalted, and the Arabs included pious phrases in their linear grilles, and even made them into mural and textile patterns.

Straightened out again, cursive lines become stripes, as they were at the start when primitive man made marks on his body and his utensils. Each of the four elements of design — Line, Shape, Texture, and Color — is continually in a state of flux, according to the dictates of fashion, and Line is the most elusive of the four. While stripes are capable of great sophistication (as in the work of the contemporary painter Gene Davis), their history is hard to trace: they are always sinking into the background of a pattern or into the alignment of its motifs. Except in the Far West. No textiles have ever surpassed Navajo blankets in the simple boldness of their bands and angles, and by going back some distance in time, and southward, we see related geometrical shapes all over the brick-faced buildings of the various Mexican and Central American cultures. The walls at Mitla, the religious center of the Zapotec Empire that flourished two thousand years ago, have reminded a recent anthropologist of "the very clear influence of basket work and weaving." Still farther south, and beginning perhaps five hundred years earlier, the dozen or so cultures of pre-conquest Peru reflect the same origins with more subtlety. There is hardly a hint of barbarism in the textiles of the Nazca, Tiahuanaco, and Chancay craftsmen. They retain the stepped triangle and sawtooth areas but often soften them by a sprinkling of small, irregular, tie-dyed squares.

Quite unexpectedly, geometry asserts itself, for the United States, in the nineteenth-century patchwork quilt. Though we know of fascinating precedents in the patches signifying token poverty on the silk robes of Buddhist priests, and in the way the Arabs and other orientals fitted diverse patterns together, patchwork as a domestic North American art form began around 1800, when our many-time-great-grandmothers practiced thrift and skill simultaneously. Genuine naïveté was not lacking, but much of it was in the patterns' names: "Kansas Trouble," "Goose in the Pond, or Young Man's Fancy," and the many variations of the "Log Cabin" arrangement, including "Courthouse Steps." Hand-

172

woven "overshot" patterns such as "Sunrise and Windows" and "Snail's Trail" were equally geometrical, but the coverlets woven more commercially on Jacquard looms tended to be highly stylized florals making frequent use of patriotic symbols.

Our rediscovery of the quilt is but a part of the ironical return of the whole art world to geometrical motifs, both plain and fancy. The plain kind first appeared during the 1920s in a form of applied Cubism called Art Moderne (later Art Deco). This style is usually attributed to the teaching of the Bauhaus in Germany (1919–1932); but aside from a lasting effect on architecture and advertising, its results were rather feeble, amounting in the decorative arts to a decade of conventionalized flora and fauna. It took Op Art, as revealed in the Museum of Modern Art's 1965 exhibit "The Responsive Eye," to awake interest in geometrical abstraction on a deeper, sometimes distressing level. Now it is a question of how far the pattern-maker can explore optical illusions — their deceptions, their vertigo — without running into difficulties.

INSPIRED IMPROVISATION. *Above*, the front of a pocketbook in needlepoint made during the 18th century in the United States. One of those instances of a specific technique, limited materials, and imagination producing a timeless curiosity, contemporary with every era that prefers angles to curves.

173

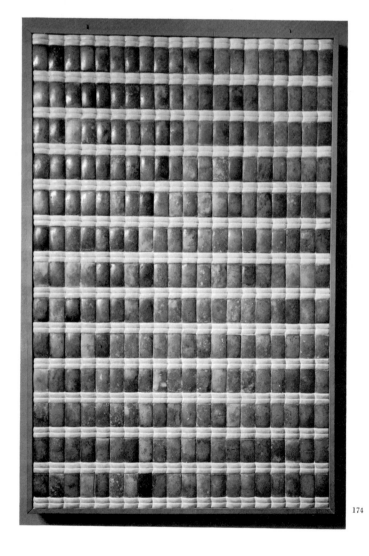

174

126

175

176

ANCIENT GEOMETRY. *Opposite, above*, portion of the mud walls imbedded with mosaic cones made from varicolored fired clay found at the Sumerian city of Ur, built around 3000 B.C. *Opposite, below*, glazed tiles from the Step Pyramid at Sakkareh, Egypt, Dynasty III, reign of Djoser, "the earliest free-standing stone structure in the world." Many of the underground passages were lined with tile — in this case brilliant turquoise blue — set in strips to recall straw matting. *Above left*, an extremely early block-printed border found at Fostat, Egypt, arresting for its cryptic arrow motif. *Above right*, square panel of a 2nd-century A.D. marble mosaic floor from Antioch that perfectly illustrates Roman Hellenism.

178

KEYS AND HOOKS. *Above, top,* a carved relief border in the church of Saint Croix at La Charité-sur-Loire, a Cluniac priory of 12th-century France. *Directly above,* an undated Shipibo Indian "beer barrel" from the upper reaches of the Amazon River. *Opposite, above,* an unidentified textile from the south coast of Peru. *Opposite, below,* a wall at Mitla, the great 13th-century religious center of the Zapotec culture near what is now Oaxaca, Mexico. Is there an obscure reason for the ubiquity of these interlocking angular motifs?

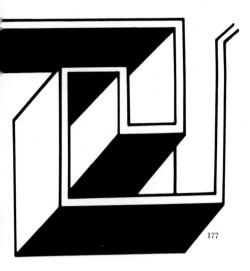

177

179

180

129

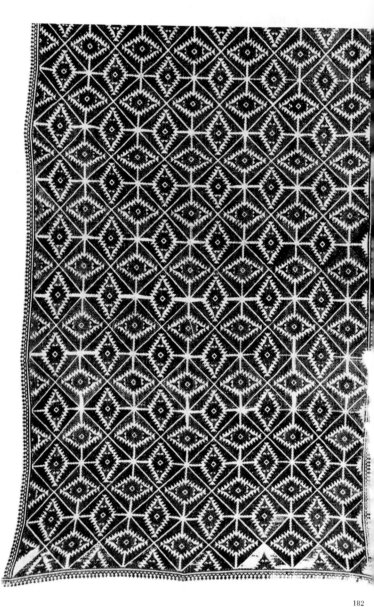

181

182

THE DIAMOND. *Above, left*, silk woven with *kara-ori*, or weft floats, from 18th-century Japan. *Above right*, an 18th-century embroidered pillow cover from the Greek island of Naxos. *Opposite*, an American Indian woman's blanket with "chief" pattern, late 19th century, in the collection of Doris Leslie Blau, New York. Not only can patterns frequently be diagrammed as contiguous "diamonds" — a strategy that combines the block and the half-drop, as on page 10 — but the motif itself is an historical favorite. See also pages 38 and 170.

183

184

TASTE VS. TRADE. *Opposite, above*, piece of cotton and rayon tunic from Nigeria, 1961. *Opposite, below*, raffia cloth with cut pile and embroidery made by the Bushcongo tribe in 19th-century Africa. *Above, top*, detail of cotton goods printed at Manchester, England, for the African market in the 1920s. *Directly above*, another pattern printed at the same time for the same market. Strangely divergent ideas are seen here. Some of the early fabrics made in Africa for Africans suggest either Art Nouveau or the severest kind of modern abstraction, while patterns manufactured for the "native market" combine everything Europe deemed "primitive," including simulated batik.

185

188

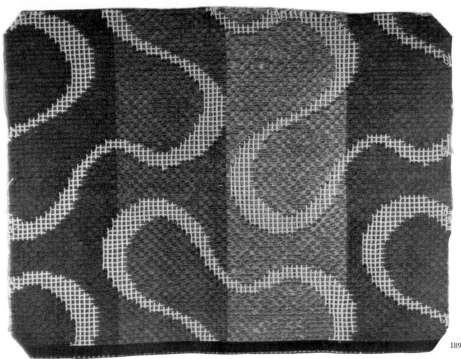

189

THE SERPENTINE. *Above, top,* a compound cloth brocaded in silk and metal from France or Spain of "Louis XV type." *Directly above,* swatch from a book of samples, France, about 1900. *Opposite, above,* section of a mid-19th-century German bookpaper. *Opposite, below,* a single width and repeat of the author's 1949 wallcovering aptly named "Mirage." The undulating lines that ornamented some of the most ancient pottery have reappeared throughout history. "Mirage" was first produced in the 3-D pressed wood-flour-and-linseed-oil German material known as lincrusta, and its interest lies in "combed" lines having been put into a repeat that can be matched and extended. See also pages 100, 105, and 109.

134

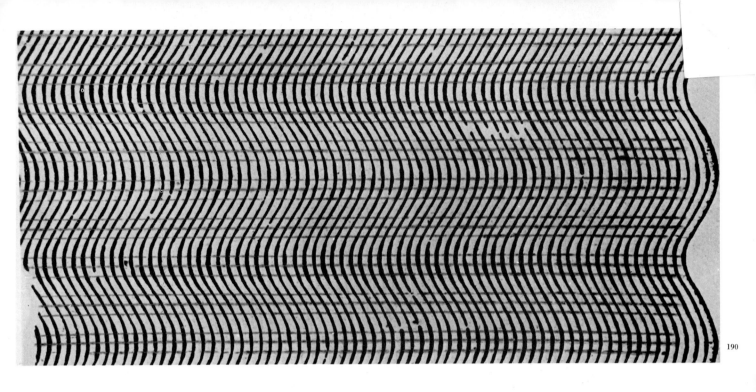

190

191

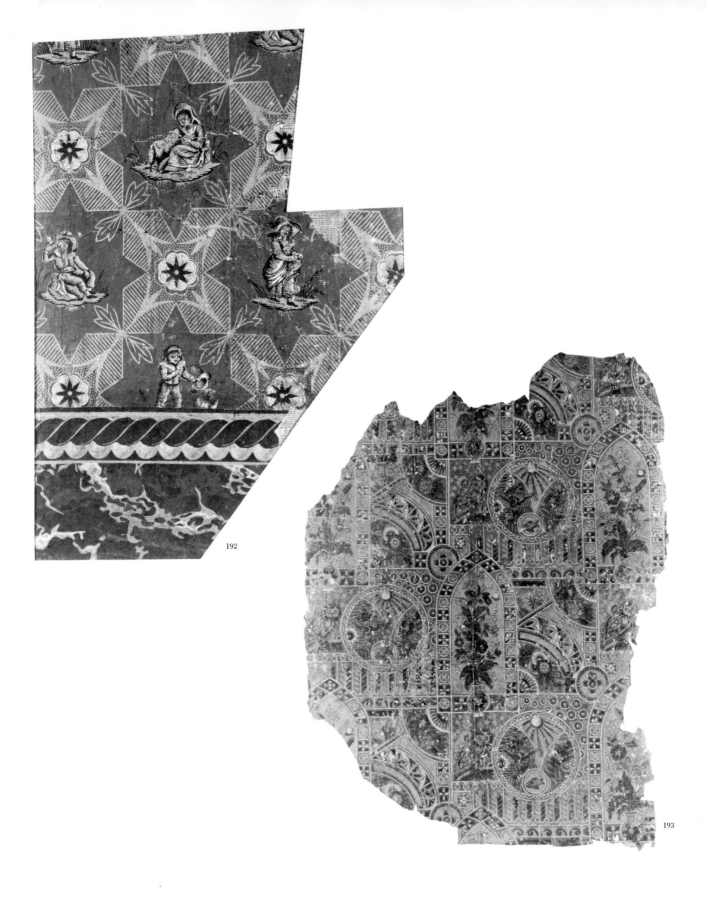

192

193

194

195

GEOMETRY DISSEMBLED. *Opposite, above,* wallpaper fragment from France, about 1800. *Opposite, below,* machine-printed wallpaper produced in the United States about 1880. *Above, top,* wallpaper of uncertain origin possibly made in the U.S. in the very early 20th century — at a period design purists hold in contempt. *Directly above,* "The Last Supper," embroidered square from an altar frontal, late 13th- or early 14th-century Lower Saxony, Germany. All these patterns are classed as Geometric, although this factor has been minimized by figurative, floral, or architectural elements. It is interesting to compare the 1880 U.S. paper with the "Leda and the Swan" *toile* on page 83, and also to observe that the leafy pinwheel, above, is called the "Princess Feather" design when used in patchwork quilts.

137

196

COVERLETS AND QUILTS. *Above left,* "Courthouse Steps," appliquéd and embroidered silk coverlet from the second half of the 19th century, United States. *Above center,* the repeating unit of a wallpaper the author adapted from a mosaic tile floor in Guatemala City, unaware that it was a well-known quilt pattern in Colonial America. *Opposite, top,* "Drunkard's Path with Sawtooth Border," from northern Michigan, about 1900. *Opposite, below,* "Baby's Blocks," a variation of the popular illusion, United States, 1920–30, unusual in its freedom of shading and the use of two shades of green, with rose. Illus-trations 198 and 199 are courtesy of Mary Strickler's Quilt Gallery, San Rafael, California.

197

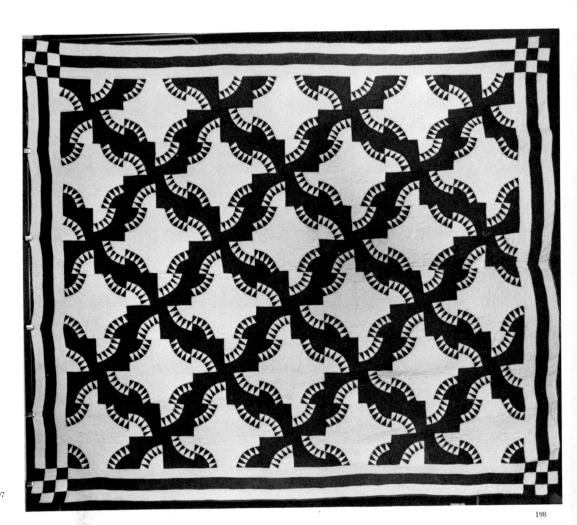

198

139

199

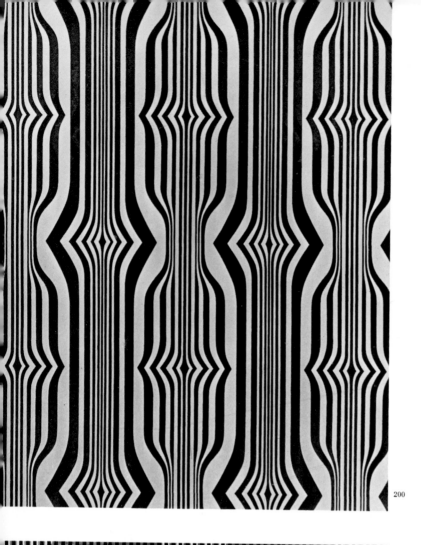

200

202

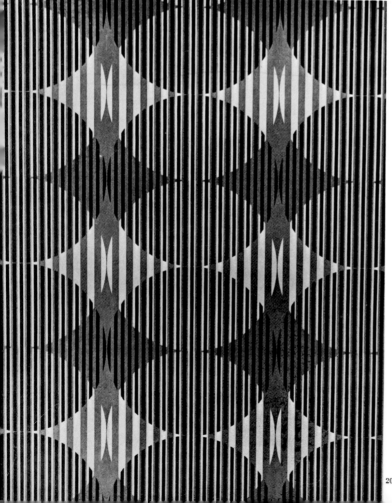

201

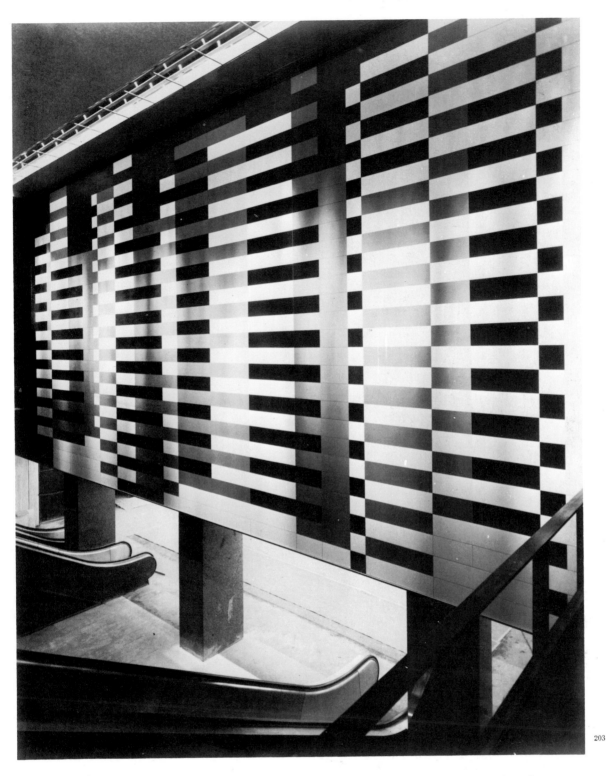

203

DAZZLERS. *Opposite, above,* "Concord," an Op Art wallpaper made in England in the late 1960s. *Opposite, below left,* "Sphere," another paper of the same description. *Opposite, below right,* "Marble Spirals," a turn-of-the-century eye-catcher from Austria that has been adapted by various U.S. manufacturers. *Above,* an oblique view of the spectacular black, white, and vermilion vinyl tile mural that Josef Albers designed in the late 1960s for the area above the bank of escalators leading to Grand Central Station from the Pan-American Building, New York City. The wallpapers were part of the Palladio 8 Collection of Arthur Sanderson and Sons Ltd., London.

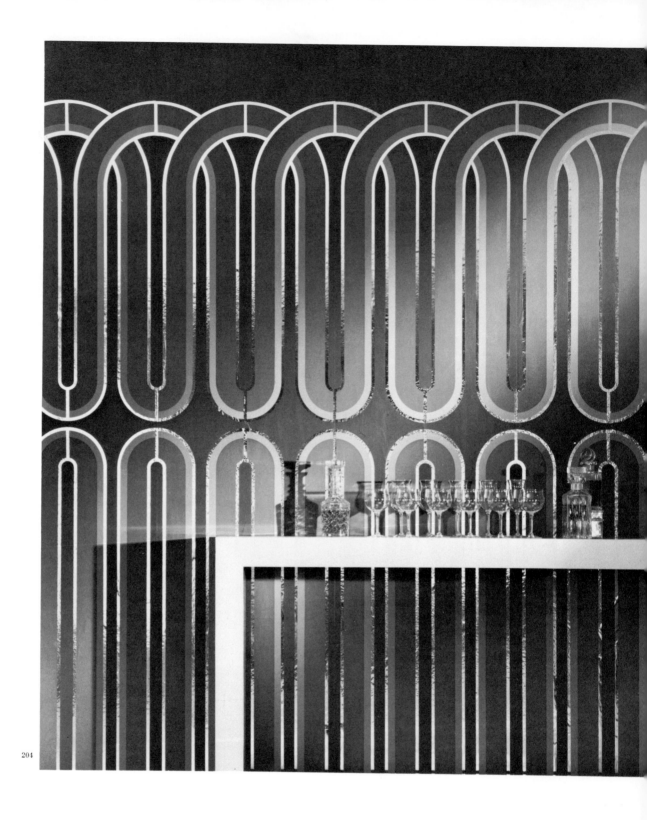

204

CONTEMPORARY DRAMA. *Above*, "Festival," a 1974 pattern by David Willson for Winfield Design Associates Inc., San Francisco. *Opposite, above*, "Adagio," by the same designer for the same firm, both wallcoverings being printed on mylar. Photographs by Jaime Ardiles-Arce. *Opposite, below*, one of a set of twelve plates produced in the late 1960s.

142

205

206

143

207

"Playthings," *above*, portion of a wallpaper for a child's room "probably France, about 1870." *Opposite*, "Balloon Ascension," an adaptation of a detail that was substituted for an animal motif "in a pattern already well established" — to record the first aerial flight of its kind, in 1783, and keep the *toiles de Jouy* timely.

208

6 Novelties

One of the fictions most cherished by the manufacturers who use pattern is that they want "something new, something different." What they want is something that sells, but, far from assuring monetary success, a novel product poses more problems than it solves. Genuine novelty always does. The resistance that originality meets with in the fine arts is, if anything, intensified in the minor, frankly commercial ones. It was the experience of the East India Company of England that the painted cottons it imported in the early seventeenth century found only a limited market until they had been "styled" to conform to English preferences for light grounds, while, at the same time, an artful, mainly unperceived reference was made to the flowering branches of England's own crewel embroidery. Hence the Tree of Life motif as we know it is substantially an Anglo-Indian invention of the middle seventeenth century, with considerable assistance from Persian miniatures and Dutch flower paintings, and the fanciful rockeries so abundant in Chinese art often form a base from which the trees could grow in what was originally a botanical-book manner. Furthermore, as I have suggested, the reason the motif of a single tree has persisted (and been ascribed, retroactively, to countless representations in remote antiquity) is that a central plant form — sacred or profane — was eminently useful to composition: first, in dividing figures and animals; later, in providing a framework for a profusion of flowers and fruit. These two types of usefulness combined to make the Tree of Life virtually evergreen.

Paisley cone motifs enjoy longevity for similar reasons. There is an apocryphal story that the bent cone originated from the imprint of a fist, made with fingers curled, resting sideways on a piece of paper after having been smeared with paint or ink. The shapes thus accounted for can easily be seen to interlock, that propensity being the motif's chief asset. Comparable adaptability is inherent in the checkerboard, the key, the scroll, the swastika, undulating or chevron stripes, and the "fish scales" called imbrication: all of them invite continuation, since they can easily cover space and as unobtrusively as desired. Yet at one time each was a novelty. Of equal weight to the theory that our decorative motifs had their origins in such domestic activities as mat weaving and pottery is the likelihood that some of them were first traced by an inspired hand whose owner may or may not have had an eye on nature. In this context it would be instructive to know how the free-forms of Jean Arp came into being. Nothing is so common in nature as the amorphous shape, but until Arp isolated it in his jigsaw constructions of painted wood it scarcely existed in art — unless it was in the "balloons" that enclose the words of comic-strip characters. Once recognized, these cloudlike areas swelled the emblems of modern art, with Henri Matisse linking them more firmly to nature by his cut-out figures and philodendron leaves, and a whole generation of North American artists adopting his flat shapes and strong colors where Matisse left off (after demonstrating his

"Strange Balustrade," *opposite*, a drawing made from a picture in what is thought to have been an album of whimsical motifs published during the past century.

mastery of the repeat in the windows he designed for the Chapel of the Rosary at Vence).

This brings patterning full circle again. Whatever its prehistoric beginnings — in home industry and subsequent diffusion, or in creative zeal and independent evolution — many centuries followed during which pattern's principal motifs and their treatment were dictated largely by painting and the sculptured bas-relief. At least that is the impression one gets from the days of the small Coptic tapestries up to and through much of the Renaissance. An especially interesting contribution was made by the Greco-Roman frescoes at Pompeii. In addition to setting precedents for the division of space and of architectural illusions, the murals exhibited a type of ornament (sometimes confusingly referred to as "arabesque") that, upon elaboration, became "trophies"; and together these delicate traceries and pictorial elements were the prime ingredients of neoclassic decoration whenever it appeared, being the sine qua non of allegorical *toiles de Jouy* with their airy scaffolding and geometrical medallions. Still other instances of skillful borrowing will be noted in the sections on Scenics and on Textures. However, some influences cannot be traced. The styles known as International Gothic and International Baroque proliferated so at random that it is impossible to say, for example, that "this motif arose from that architectural practice," for it could just as well be the other way around: a device appearing in pattern form prior to being embodied in a church or palace.

So much for originality of style. In this regard the fine and the popular arts may always have influenced each other; we simply do not know to what degree. Nor — when it comes to subject matter — are we certain of their relative response to current events, since the art objects of the common man tend to be perishable, and enduring monuments are comparatively rare. Indeed, ephemera in great quantity do not exist much before the nineteenth century, when inexpensive methods of manufacture made it feasible to produce cheap souvenirs of public occasions. Battles, anniversaries, balloon ascensions, and the dedication of canals and railways were excuses for articles equivalent to the current spate of "commemorative" postage stamps, coins, and other objects, man being an inveterate collector.

Our own century is grossly overdocumented. In the seventies we are even now being asked to look on the fifties with nostalgia, while the memorabilia of the twenties and thirties approach the status of incunabula and pre-Columbian gold. A program of sharp appraisal is consequently imminent, for there can be no question that many twentieth-century products are worthless, and are being saved from the junk heap principally because we choose to ignore the fact that most objects from the distant past have survived, not for any vaguely mawkish reasons but because they possess genuine merit. As the musuems fill to overflowing it is absurd to suppose that today's horrors will necessarily be tomorrow's treasures.

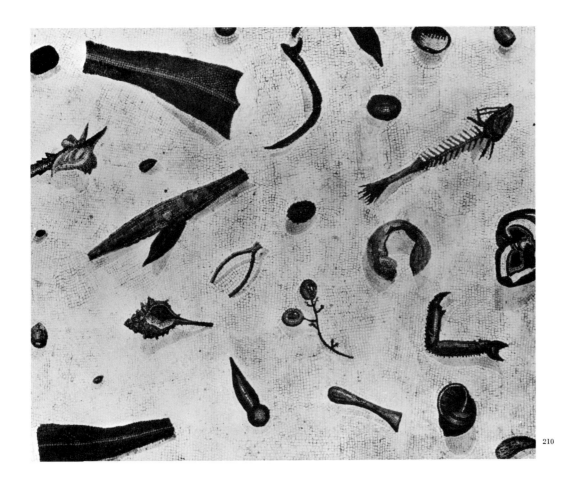

Its curiosities perhaps. Occasionally a style does appear which demands that standard criticism be held in abeyance. Art Nouveau was such a style, and Art Deco tried valiantly to achieve distinction (but found the fusion of Cubism and naturalism discouraging). Shortly afterward, in the forties, a nameless but quite definite renaissance of taste was made possible by three factors: the perfecting of silkscreen printing, a shortage of raw materials due to World War II, and the presence, in New York, of many spirited and talented persons from Europe. Against austere backgrounds, dressed in simple clothes, a brief era of elegance ensued, at once creative and self-critical — for the two faculties are at their best when combined. The decorative luxuries produced at the time naturally reflected the schools of Surrealist or Neo-Romantic painting then in favor. Novelties, as has been observed, are a recurrent phenomenon. Those of the forties were dubbed "conversation pieces" and they were deemed successful insofar as they showed imagination and wit.

"The Unswept Floor," *above*, a detail of an ancient mosaic in the Lateran Museum, Rome, which in all likelihood was meant as an amusing comment on the table manners that prevailed among Romans of every class.

211

THE LEGACY OF POMPEII. *Above*, mural fragment in the Third Pompeiian Style. *Opposite, left,* section of what is called a "slender repeating arabesque, Grotesque design," France, about 1800. *Opposite, above right,* watercolor drawing for a wall decoration, Italy, 1825–50. *Opposite, below right,* "trophy" designs by Jean Charles Delafosse (1734–89). Interpretations of the wall paintings at Pompeii lost much of their majesty over the centuries, being gradually reduced to theatrical scenery, to groups of symbolical objects, and to what, today, we might call "assemblage."

150

212

213

214

215

216

217

MARQUETRY AND LACQUER. *Opposite, above,* the base of a marquetry cabinet from Germany, about 1740. *Opposite, below,* detail of the tier of drawers at the right. *Above,* free adaptation of the top of a lacquer box from 12th-century Japan with a design of partly submerged cart wheels, which were periodically soaked to keep them from cracking.

MEN AND THEIR INVENTIONS. *Above*, panel of machine-made lace, France, about 1900. *Opposite, above*, "General Hoche," woodblock-printed wallpaper, Paris, about 1799. *Opposite, below*, "General Washington in a Masonic triangle," a wallpaper of the post-Revolutionary period, United States. Both wallpapers courtesy of Mary E. Dunn, President, Nancy McClelland, Inc. Industrial and portrait subjects are equally rare in pattern design. The locomotive-and-balloon subject, being in black lace, was doubtless intended as an overskirt.

154

218

219

220

221

222

223

HIGH FASHION. *Above, top,* project for embroidery by the busy J. B. Bony, France, about 1790. *Above, middle,* project for a woven border by an unknown French artist, 1805–15. *Directly above,* salesman's sample of embroidery "in the manner of" M. Bony. *Opposite, above,* design for an embroidered coat lapel by Mlle. Matalon, "probably at Lyon, about 1788." *Opposite, below,* another embroidered waistcoat design, 1780–90. Fashions at all times depend upon novelty, and nowhere more so than in France.

156

224

225

226

227

228

229

230

IN RETROSPECT. *Opposite, above left*, "Skeletons." *Opposite, above right*, "Parasols in the Wind." *Opposite, below*, "Ginger Jar." *Above left*, "Cloud Brocade." *Above right*, "Shore Leave." These five patterns span nearly forty years of the author's work in the field of decorative furnishing design, beginning with the 1936 "closet" paper (opposite, above left), and ending with the novelty based on twenty-odd tattooing motifs, from a 1968 collection called "Avatars." The two patterns shown in the center belonged to different yearly collections, although both of them, like the bamboo pattern on page 118, betray a penchant for simplified *chinoiserie*.

231

"The Brooklyn Bridge paper," *above*, can hardly be imagined as covering living room walls, but may well have been made for what are called "display" papers — although, again, by including still-life, floral, and other landscape motifs the manufacturer may have sought a wider market. Surely it dates from around 1883, when the big bridge was completed. *Opposite*, the focal point of the most famous scenic textile from 14th-century Lucca, pieces of which exist (as do many patterns) in a number of museums.

160

232

7 Scenics

Considering how popular it was to become, landscape painting as a separate genre got off to a late start, landscape patterns even later. Assyrian sculptors had used out-of-door settings for their bas-reliefs, as had journeymen painters of the less regal Egyptian tombs, but always as a background for figures. After an exuberant period when Roman villas displayed scenic effects in four styles of increasingly theatrical decoration, Byzantine mosaics confined themselves to employing bits of landscape or architecture as mere props, as what Sir Kenneth Clark calls landscape symbols. In *Landscape into Art* he writes that St. Anselm, in the twelfth century, thought that things were harmful "in proportion to the senses they delighted," and therefore that it was "dangerous" to sit in a garden where roses were in bloom, Sir Kenneth adding his own observation, "This no doubt expresses the strictest monastic view. The average man would not have thought it wrong to enjoy nature; he would simply have said that nature was unenjoyable."

Such an attitude was exclusively western. While the medieval West slowly grew reconciled to Nature, the medieval East began to edit it, so to speak: the Japanese in connection with the tea ceremony that changed their entire culture, the Persians by planting gardens that heralded their painted miniatures, "paradise" being the Persian term for "a walled enclosure." As with the early appearance of animals in textile design, the gradual release of landscape from confining shapes — from roundels or cartouches — was a big step in making patterns less formal. Another boon to their popular favor was the development, in every country of the East and the Near East, of diverse types of brushwork, all of which led to a facility in writing and drawing, with floral and landscape painting an extension of calligraphy. And because the landscapes of the East were executed on scrolls or for albums, and were not meant to be framed (as western pictures are), this freedom from boundaries was of much benefit in showing how a repeated scene need not look like "just one bad picture after another."

We are first conscious of scenic elements grouped into small vignettes in the textiles woven in the city republic of Lucca in central Italy early in the fourteenth century. It is probable that this compositional device came from China, as did the phoenixes, winged dragons, and the deerlike horses (or unicorns) called *kh'i-lin*. Mongol conquests in the Near East are said to have brought all manner of Chinese goods closer to Europe, and it is my belief that the "glory of rays," which, above all else, distinguish Luccan patterns, were not merely flames or sunbursts borrowed from the Orient, but were a sign of the Italian piety that, several centuries later, was to reassert itself in the extravagance of the Baroque period (e.g., in the sculpture of Giovanni Lorenzo Bernini, 1598–1680). Shortly afterward the Baroque became Rococo and secular. The weavers of Lucca having long since fled tyranny in their own city and gone to Venice,

A ROMAN MURAL. *Opposite*, a 1st-century wallpainting found at Boscoreale, a suburb of Pompeii. This single section of a small sitting room or "cubiculum" combines all four styles of Pompeiian decoration — "Encrusted," "Architectural," "Ornate," and "Intricate" — generally believed to have been painted mostly by artists from Greece.

163

where they introduced weaving in silk, it is altogether likely that, at the beginning of the eighteenth century, they added their flair for fantasy to the mysterious Bizarre Silks that were almost certainly produced at orientalized Venice during the brief years they were at their strangest.

Back in Persia, meanwhile, patterned landscapes had become as familiar as the neatly spaced rows of flowers or plants we think of as more typically Persian. Granted that the suspended mountains of the best Chinese and Japanese painting had a poetic and philosophical content that Persian art never approached, the artists of Persia were always superlative designers, and never more so than during the sixteenth and seventeenth century of the Safavid Dynasty. As the Greeks a dozen centuries before had been craftsmen-in-residence to the Mediterranean world, the Persians now went wherever their Islamic conquerors commanded them, impressing subtleties of color and design on products throughout India, Turkey, and Spain. Up to the end of the nineteenth century it is an exceptional group of tiles, textiles, rugs, or carpets from Europe or America that does not have something Persian about it.

The cotton hangings painted in India and the shawls woven there, at Kashmir, have been discussed. A less obvious example of Persian influence is that made on western industry in the field of printed yardage, called *toiles de Jouy* after the factory on the river Bièvre, near Versailles, that was established by Christophe-Philippe Oberkampf in 1760. Rarely are the subjects oriental — unless inspired by the designs of Jean-Baptiste Pillement (1719–1808) — rarely are the compositions anything else. What I have described as "floating islands" made it possible to combine a number of distinct scenes by leaving irregular edges around them, as if they were jottings in a notebook, or vistas cut off by mist. Too mundane to recall a similar strategy in the blazing visions of Lucca, they are more readily traced to the swift notations made on the less expensive Chinese dishes, lacquer trays, or fans since, during the eighteenth century, the European craze for *chinoiserie* (whatever the actual country of origin!) was at its height. In China itself xenophophia waxed and waned. It should be noted, furthermore, that we were then, as perhaps we are now, considered barbarians. Those countless sets of panels the Chinese painted with flowering vines and tiny birds for rich houses in England, France, and North America were never used in their own homes. When the people of the Far East desired an outdoor atmosphere, they preferred to suggest it by the restrained use of screens and scrolls.

It may have been a matter of technique as much as taste. Tempera and oil painting in Europe had fostered first the small and then the large landscape, with the great gardeners from at least Renaissance times onward going directly to the fine arts for the impression they wished to create. Marie Luise Gothein's *A History of Garden Art* recounts in detail the debt owed to such painters as Nicolas Poussin (1594–1655), Claude Lorrain (1600–1682), and even the satirist William Hogarth (1697–1764), whose famous "line of beauty" presumably gave the landscapist Capability Brown — so nicknamed because "he was forever

talking about the 'capabilities' of his garden grounds" — the idea of curving banks of water so that, as he claimed, "the Thames will never forgive me." This question left unsettled, it is evident that men who could afford gardens complete with artificial ruins in which to cultivate melancholy (as proposed by Jean-Jacques Rousseau) could afford continuous panels of wallpaper that took several years and several thousand blocks to print. These handsome productions of the early nineteenth century, which Nancy McClelland called "the great age of scenics," were in no sense patterns; they were indeed thought to have been suggested by the cycloramas that were a favorite public entertainment. Their importance to us lies in what the English call "tone" and we refer to as value. Without resorting to shading, all the great scenics achieve a discreet degree of depth by means of a posterlike definition every pattern should possess.

THE ROYAL PAVILION, BRIGHTON. *Above*, a design in tempera for the music room of the Prince Regent (later George IV) by Frederick Crace (1779–1859) and executed "with slight differences in detail" in 1822. First conceived in pseudo–East Indian taste — still maintained on the exterior — the Royal Pavilion is perhaps the world's most beguiling monument to eclecticism.

165

235

THREE GARDENS. *Above*, a wool carpet from northwest Persia or Kurdistan, 1700–50, with highly stylized pools and beds of flowers. *Opposite, above*, "Fêtes Greques," from the Nancy McClelland collection of paper murals hand-blocked during "the great age of scenics" of the early 19th century. Photograph courtesy of Mary E. Dunn. *Opposite, below*, small detail of one of the papers painted in China during the 18th century for export to Europe, where they profoundly influenced decorative styles from Portugal to Russia.

166

236

237

238

239

240

241

MADE IN ENGLAND. *Opposite, above,* a copperplate printed in red on natural cotton, designed by Pillement during a sojourn in England. *Opposite, below,* "Outdoor Sports and Pastimes," also a copperplate print — in sepia — by an anonymous English designer about 1790. *Above, top,* "Captain Cook's Voyage," still another print on cotton from England, about 1780. *Directly above,* detail of the same. Each of these patterns being of the *toiles de Jouy* type, and produced in the same country within a few decades, the difference in the way each one covers space is quite surprising. For further "toile" variations see pages 82 and 83.

169

242

243

244

PICTURES AS PATTERN. *Opposite, above,* an odd attempt to transform four diamond-shaped pictures of children at play into a pattern by suggesting upholstered patchwork — a textile printed in late 19th-century United States. *Opposite, below,* "Scenes in Canada," a wallpaper printed by machine in England, in 1860, and chiefly interesting as a perfect example of the "brick" repeat. *Above,* "The Print Room," Woodhall Park, Hertfordshire, England, photograph courtesy of Mr. P. H. Sidney, the present lessee, and copyrighted by the magazine *Country Life* — an outstanding example of the 18th- and 19th-century custom of decorating suitable rooms with prints "framed" by paper borders.

243

RAOUL DUFY, PAINTER-DESIGNER. *Above*, "The Thresher," a printed cotton designed by Dufy in France about 1930. *Opposite, above*, "La Pêche," a woodcut made as a book illustration in 1911. *Opposite, below*, "Reclining Nude," gouache on paper, dated 1930. The artist seems to have developed his characteristic calligraphic line from knife slashes which, in his more serious later work, were overlaid with flat washes of color that became one of the most widely used — and abused — devices of modernism.

172

246

247

173

248

THE TOUR DE FORCE. *Above*, an exceptionally sumptuous wallpaper border printed from woodblocks in France, 1805–15. *Opposite*, this corn motif of metal thread and pearl beads was embroidered in the United States in 1940.

249

8 Textures

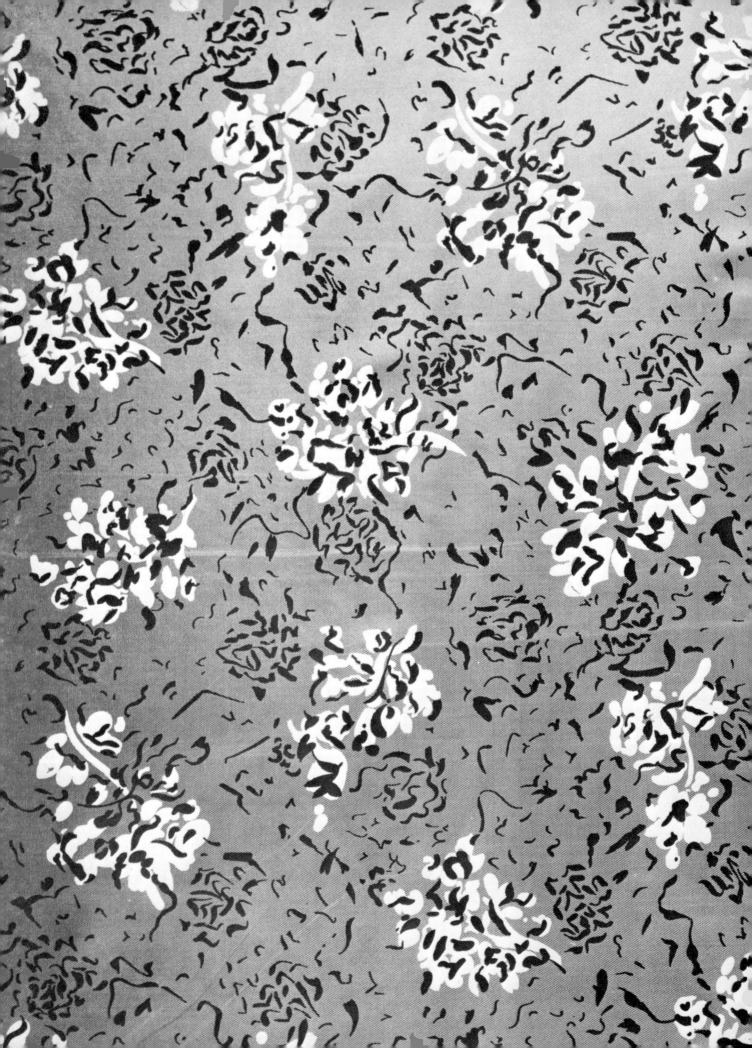

It could be argued that Texture is not pattern at all, but the surface of a material, or the result of a technique. Ambiguous as the categories of motifs frequently are, in this one subject matter, as such, is irrelevant; sheer physical quality — or its simulation — is what counts. Previous standards become meaningless. To what avail do we know that good patterns are neither cluttered nor sparse; that each line and shape within an admirable pattern must be related and serve a purpose? Guidance from the fine arts is especially disconcerting. With their long tradition of realistic deception, and the current tendency of art to parody itself (and the ages), we would be wise to seek a more forthright guide to what is genuine and worth attention.

Forgery as it is practiced in painting and sculpture is seldom at issue. We understand that wealthy Egyptians, Greeks, and Romans collected ancient objects and some of them were found to be fraudulent. In his book *Fakes*, Otto Kurtz makes an instructive distinction. Although he does not begin the story of known art forgeries until the fifteenth century, he reminds us that copies of early works were not intended, originally, to deceive: that enterprise arose later, through the efforts of jealous artists or unscrupulous restorers. Items of purely decorative art, being less valuable, either escaped scrutiny or their incongruities lent them charm. Transparent imitation has in fact been one of the tricks that sophisticated decoration found "amusing." Panels or pillars of wood painted to resemble marble are among the charms of many Italian churches, and by odd coincidence the whole wallpaper industry began in sixteenth-century France when a guild of "domino makers" turned to producing sheets of marbleized paper to cover boxes and line books — by a flotation technique believed to have originated in Turkey. When we add the handpainted floral scenics from China to our sources, we appreciate the number of countries that have contributed to what is now a spectacular business. And the heart of its success is mimicry.

Which is also the mainspring of fashion. More interested in appearance than in necessity, fashion strains for novelty, celebrates success by launching a new perfume, and wryly suffers the flattery of tawdry emulation. Texture and texturing enter the picture at every stage. If a fashion begins with natural, costly materials, artificial, cheap ones are rapidly found to replace them, as flocked wallpaper replaced hangings made of cloth. Sometimes the procedure was reversed. If a queen made cotton fashionable, its simple figurations were duplicated in silk, much as, today, the Indian weavers of Guatemala substitute shiny rayon for the cotton thread that made their native fabrics desirable. Since style chiefly depends upon the quality of the material that is used, it will be apparent to what extent the plastic age we live in has fomented well-nigh universal confusion.

"Printed Silk," *opposite*, an apparel fabric by Stephanie Cartwright, United States, 1953. Although at first glance a "design by accident," the splattered shapes conceal a floral motif in a pattern that has a definite repeat: note that a motif just right of center, toward the top, and a motif at the lower left are identical.

For old habits outlast their need. There were practical reasons why many classes of historical patterns used dense coverage or broken surfaces: for one, they didn't show dirt so much in the dark ages before detergents and dry-cleaning. To review pattern principally as it originated in textiles or quasi-textiles — where every motif and manner of repeat eventually appears — we recall that a process known as mimesis continued the stitches made in animal hides for the decorative marks on pottery, and that plaited rush mats instituted any number of geometrical motifs that were later used architecturally and in mosaics. The gradual sophistication and mechanization of weaving methods also contributed their share; all this, while man's own imagination added fanciful elements to those obviously evolved from home and commercial industry. Styles in dress must not be forgotten. Voluminous garments required large-scaled patterns (or vice versa), and, on the other hand, the sumptuary laws that were passed from time to time in every affluent country provided both an ostensible check upon, and an incentive to, the luxurious display that signals civilization. Nor must we forget how quickly we human beings are bored. From my own limited observation, only the nations greatest in design seem to have clung to a sensible mode of dress once they achieved it. The clothes of the Egyptians and the Chinese remained basically unchanged century after century.

Novel textures were first confined to royalty. Silk is the prime example, but every court wore the finest furs or plumage available — the Incas whole mantles of feathers. But the real culprit for excessive embellishment was the embroiderer's needle, that apparently innocent instrument that could not abide an empty space. There are mildly cautionary specimens on page 194 and 195. (As a matter of discretion we have excluded horrible examples of pattern or technique, though occasionally they would have been helpful.) When it was seen that a brocaded damask — so typical of Bizarre Silks — created an illusion of depth by showing, as on two distinct planes, one pattern above another, texture entered a new phase, weakening more patterns than were aided. This was *horror vacui* with a vengeance. Even a designer of the stature of William Morris gave some of his handsomest large florals an entirely gratuitous background motif. The patterns are vastly improved if it is eliminated. Indeed, many of the secondary motifs in historical textiles could be beneficially removed, thus providing the minute filigree type of pattern present-day manufacturers often call "textures" — to imply that they have no character of their own. To my knowledge only the French have habitually used stripes as an integral second motif, by this means supporting sprays of flowers at once logically and with detachment.

All these impulses are readily understood. Most of them have merit — or some merit can be extracted. The only truly reprehensible abuse of texture occurred in this century, possibly touched off quite inadvertently by the luxurious, ancient-looking fabrics a Venetian of noble family named Fortuny developed by a still "secret" process that must originally have involved printing pigments

251

on silk with rather crudely carved woodblocks. As Fortuny's designs dated
mainly from the Renaissance, and their prestige was enormous, most of the
western world's commercial textiles used for furnishing soon bore a strong re-
semblance to threadbare damask. And one abuse of texture led to another.
Sensing that many of the designs offered them were of poor quality, and convinced that the public equated indistinct images with elegance, the manufacturers acquired a habit of "mucking up" a pattern, good or bad, either by printing it on a coarse ground or an unusual material, or by specifying a "dry brush"
rendering that softened any definite outlines or shapes. In some quarters these
evasions continue, with all heads buried in texture up to their necks. Elsewhere
the prospect for clean-cut design, regardless of period connotation, constantly
brightens. After all, every pattern was positive, was contemporary, when it
was designed.

"Poncho Shirt with feather application," *above*, an incredible survival from the Chimu
culture of Peru.

252

253

254

MARBLE AND MOSAIC. *Opposite, above,* a "classical" design for the Royal Pavilion, Brighton, by Frederick Crace, for whose *chinoiserie* see page 165. *Opposite, below,* section of "Byzantium," one of the author's rotogravure wallpapers, photographed from *tesserae* imbedded in mortar. *Above,* a general view of the 5th-century basilica of S. Vitale, Ravenna, Italy, the interior of which is an encyclopedia of Hellenistic and Near Eastern design motifs and patterns executed in a wide range of costly materials.

255

LEATHER, WOOD, AND LACE. *Above,* an embossed, painted, and gilded "Cordova" leather wallcovering of the 16th century in a room at the Rijksmuseum, Amsterdam. *Opposite, above,* simulated woodgrain of a wallpaper printed by the intaglio or engraved-roller process in the United States, 1890–1900. *Opposite, below,* an exceptionally exquisite handkerchief bordered with "Argenteuil" lace.

256

257

258

FEATHERS AND FUR. *Above,* watercolor design for the panel of a "feather skirt" by an unknown artist at Lyon, 1785–90. See also pages 156, 157. *Opposite, above,* section of a silk and chenille brocaded cape from the second half of the 18th century, France. *Opposite, below,* ribbed moire silk brocaded with "ostrich plume" stripes, France, about 1870. Fine feathers and fur — real or simulated — connote luxury, whatever the period.

184

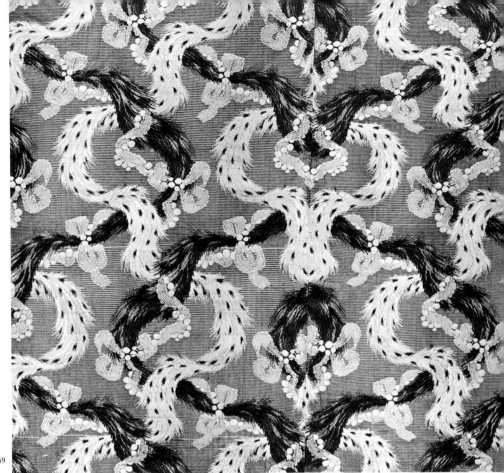

259

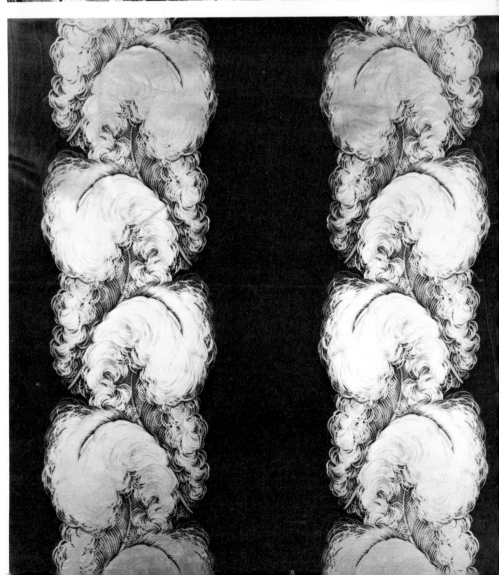

261

262

263

264

OUT OF THE EARTH. *Opposite, above left,* an Islamic wall panel of carved stucco. *Opposite, below,* similar arabesques, converted to ceramic, adapted with great skill to the curved dome of a mosque. *Above center,* four tiles which, put together, form the sunburst motif so often found in open grillwork. See page 12 for the method used to construct designs of this kind. *Directly above,* by way of complete contrast, a porcelain plate with an overglaze decoration by Francis Lycett, painted in New York in 1890.

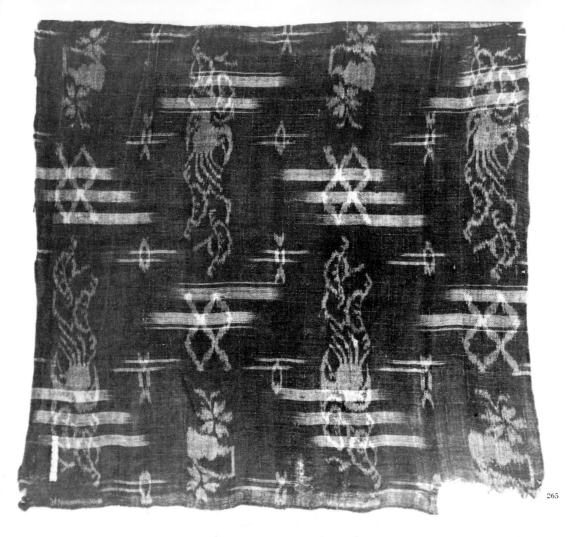

265

266

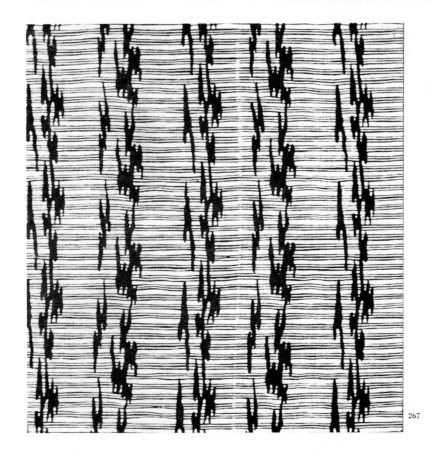

267

268

TRUE AND IMITATION IKAT. *Opposite, above,* a piece of "Kasuri cloth" from early 19th-century Japan. *Opposite, below,* section of a comparable fabric with both warp and weft tie-dyed threads as still woven by the native Indians of Guatemala, who lay out the desired pattern between sticks in any large open area. *Above, top,* a Japanese cotton printed to suggest that the warp has been patterned by tie-dyeing. *Directly above,* another print made in France with the same deception in mind. The term "ikat" is Indonesian, but weavers in any number of countries, including Spain, make use of thread to obtain a shadowy effect either by previously spot-dyeing it or by painting the warp when it is on the loom.

270

269

A MATTER OF SCALE. *Above left*, dress yardage shown in an advertisement with a portrait of the singer Jenny Lind (1820–87). *Above right*, an enlarged detail of the small pattern — perhaps intended as a vine; actually a species of the wormlike tracery called "vermiculation," which was frequently employed to break up flat surfaces in Renaissance masonry. *Opposite, above*, an Islamic pattern (from the same source as those on page 12) that becomes a Texture by reason of its delicacy. *Opposite, center*, composite of a canvas by Julio Le Parc, exhibited in the late 1960s at the Howard Wise Gallery in New York. The painting has been repeated four times to create a vibrant surface that could easily be woven by an expert, since all areas have right angles. *Opposite, below*, the author's wallcovering "Cosmati," much reduced in scale to make a quasi-organic pattern based on triangles.

271

272

273

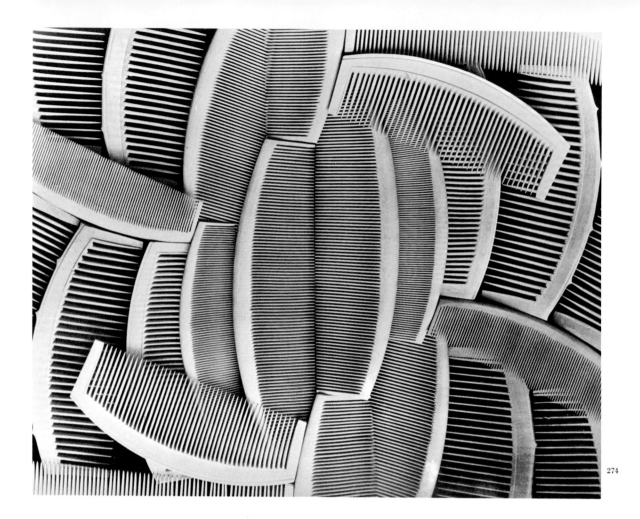

274

275

PATTERNS BY PHOTOGRAPHY. *Above, top,* "Japanese Wooden Combs." *Directly above,* "Jelly Molds." *Opposite, above,* "Craters on the Moon" (egg crates). *Opposite, below,* "House of Cards," detail. These are the remnants of some fifty patterns the author devised from common objects when working with the Los Angeles photographer Margrethe Mather during 1922–30 toward eventual exhibition at the De Young Museum in Golden Gate Park, San Francisco. Several of the subjects were produced commercially by various engraving processes, but the new "transfer" techniques would make photographic pattern reproduction — on all surfaces — more feasible today.

192

276

277

278

279

280

OLD EMBROIDERY AND NEW. *Opposite, above,* "Black-work," part of a pillow cover embroidered in the fashionable 16th- and 17th-century style of black silk on light linen, England. *Opposite, below,* detail of a Noh robe from late 16th-century, Japan. *Above,* panel of palm fiber worked in various threads by Mariska Karasz, United States, about 1950. For very different embroidery techniques see pages 63, 132, and 137.

281

282

283

OLD TAPESTRY AND NEW. *Opposite, above,* "The Feudal Life," a 15th-century wool tapestry from Touraine, France, replete with figure and animal subjects on a richly varied *millefleurs* background. See page 95 for a comparable detail, early as it is. *Opposite, below,* "Profiles," wool, synthetic fibers and novelty yarn in a tapestry-weave hanging by Eva Anttila, Finland, 1952. *Above,* an abstract wall hanging of various fibers with insets of acrylic plastic woven by Ted Hallman, United States, 1962.

Bibliography

Escher, M. C. *The Graphic Work of M. C. Escher.* Translated from the Dutch by John E. Brigham. New York: Meredith Press, 1967. Other publications of Escher's "periodic drawings" and similar works that defy normal procedures in composition and perspective are available, but this is the most comprehensive book in English. As regards pattern design, Escher's command of distortion and his penchant for strange subject matter may or may not be influential. Further experiment along the lines he has indicated will require both tremendous technical dexterity and a certain tastefulness this amazing Dutchman frequently lacked.

Gardner, Helen. *Gardner's Art through the Ages.* Sixth edition revised by Horst de la Croix and Richard G. Tansy. New York: Harcourt Brace Jovanovich, 1975.

Those who grew up with this textbook, first published in 1926, will not recognize it in its latest incarnation. After an Introduction that treats of styles and techniques, the twenty-two chapters range from the Stone Age in Western Europe through international trends in the twentieth century, and include sections on the arts of India, China, and Japan, as well as those of Central and South America, Africa, and Oceania. The many maps and diagrams are especially helpful, for, with the hundreds of illustrations, they keep the reader constantly oriented. A ten-page Glossary and an extensive Bibliography make this perhaps the most useful single book on art history, providing a framework for further study in any field of esthetics.

Irwin, John, and Katharine B. Brett. *Origins of Chintz, With a catalogue of Indo-European cotton-paintings in the Victoria and Albert Museum, London, and the Royal Ontario Museum, Toronto.* London: Her Majesty's Stationery Office, 1970.

Mr. Irwin, Keeper of the Oriental section at the Victoria and Albert Museum, is known among textile historians for "reversing the trade winds," some years ago, by proving the European origin of many of the "exotic" motifs in merchandise made for the several East India Companies beginning at the end of the sixteenth century. The present volume is at once handsome, entertaining, and of impeccable scholarship.

Lee, Sherman E. *A History of Far Eastern Art.* New York: Abrams, 1964.

It would be hard to imagine a more beautiful and thorough presentation of a vast subject than this volume by the Director of the Cleveland Museum of Art, who is also its Curator of Oriental Art. There are now a number of impressive oriental collections in the United States, but one of the distinctions of this book is that about half of its illustrations are of superb works still in the Far East.

Mayer-Thurman, Christa C. *Masterpieces of Western Textiles, from The Art Institute of Chicago.* First published in 1969, soon to be enlarged and reprinted.

An excellent paperbound book, compiled by the Curator of Textiles, which is also a condensed textbook of the subject. Many of the great museums publish cross-sections of world art based on their own collections, and at times issue exhibition catalogues that become invaluable. This is a prime example of the custom, notable for its discriminating selection from abundant and unusual material.

Noma, Seiroku. *Japanese Costume and Textile Arts.* Volume 16 of The Heibonsha Survey of Japanese Art. New York: John Weatherhill, joint publisher with Heibonshu, Tokyo, 1974.

Certainly the largest number of extraordinary patterns ever gathered in one small book. A marvelous bargain for the contemporary designer who — it will be hoped — exercises taste commensurate with the inspiration provided within these pages.

Schmutzler, Robert. *Art Nouveau.* New York: Abrams, 1965.

By embracing every possible "contribution" to what was in reality a short-lived style, Mr. Schmutzler's large book — a great bargain in paperback — constitutes an engrossing review of some of the most original visual images artists have projected in the past one hundred and fifty years, although the emphasis, very properly, is on the decade that bridged the nineteenth and twentieth centuries.

Taggart, Ross E., chief editor. *Handbook, Nelson Gallery of Art and Atkins Museum of Fine Arts.* Fifth edition in two boxed volumes, hardcover or paperbound. Kansas City, Mo.: 1973.

On its fortieth anniversary this institution presented its treasures in a new format that separates the Occident from the Orient and adds up to a comprehensive history of art — brilliant in its directness. Every museum buff looks at and buys special books and "souvenirs" from the shops located near the entrance of most museums. Here is a unique addition to any art addict's library.

Thornton, Peter. *Baroque and Rococo Silks.* London: Faber and Faber, 1965.

Mr. Thornton is another member of the staff at the Victoria and Albert Museum (where he is currently Keeper of Woodworking), but this delightful and scholarly work is not an official "V&A" publication; it also draws heavily on a number of sources including Scandinavian collections and the Musée Historique des Tissus at Lyons, France. Seventeenth- and eighteenth-century silks offer a fantastic array of patterns — once again to be approached with discretion, for the inventions of French textile designers (in particular) are surpassed in audacity only by the ingenious Japanese.

Weibel, Adèle Coulin. *Two Thousand Years of Textiles (The Figured Textiles of Europe and the Near East).* New York: Pantheon, 1952, published for the Detroit Institute of Arts.

For nearly a quarter of a century this has been the indispensable guide in English to textiles as a whole. "Pattern" and "textile" are not necessarily synonymous, and this survey emphasizes antiquity and weaving techniques rather than interesting design, but its historical value is beyond question.

"Daisy Egg." A pattern freely drawn in India ink by Kristin Chiara, 1975.

INDEX

(Numerals in *italics* indicate illustrations)

201

Sources of Photographs

The numbered photographs not identified in captions or text are by the much-appreciated courtesy of the following institutions:

Art Institute of Chicago: 17 29, 30, 36, 59, 98, 107, 179, 195, 238, 239, 242, 251, 259, 281; Benaki Museum, Athens: 22; The Brooklyn Museum: 240; Cooper–Hewitt Museum of Design, Smithsonian Institution: 20, 23, 31, 32, 40, 43-46, 48, 49-56, 60-62, 66, 67, 81, 85, 87-90, 104-06, 109-11, 113, 115, 117, 124, 135, 136, 139, 142, 148, 150-54, 156, 161-65, 169, 171, 172, 175, 184-90, 192, 194, 206, 207, 212-14, 219, 221-25, 231, 234, 243, 245, 247, 248, 250, 252, 256, 258, 260, 264, 265, 268, 269, 278-80, 282, 283; The Metropolitan Museum of Art: 36, 75, 76, 86, 92, 102, 108, 146, 147, 174, 176, 181, 218, 233, 235; Musée des Arts Decoratifs, Paris: 12; Musée Historique des Tissus de Lyon: 47, 140, 257; Museo Poldi–Pezzoli, Milan: 147; Museum of Art, Rhode Island School of Design: 211; Museum of Fine Arts, Boston: frontispiece, 19, 74, 96, 101, 138, 145; Museum of Primitive Art, New York: 69; Nelson Gallery–Atkins Museum, Kansas City, Mo.: 68, 94, 95, 149, 215; Rijksmuseum: 255; The Textile Museum, Washington, D.C.: 100, 128, 129; Victoria & Albert Museum (Crown Copyright): 42, 70, 71, 144, 155, 157, 158, 237.